Slouching Toward Catastrophe

How the Obama Administration's Defense Policies Jeopardize America and the Free World

By David M. Walsh, Ph.D

TABLE OF CONTENTS.

Prologue--2015: The Next World War.

With hindsight, the world war that began barely a month ago was all but inevitable. The wave of revolutions that swept the Middle East beginning in 2010--the so-called "Arab Spring"--created a vast power vacuum across the region. The power benefitting most from this upheaval was Iran. The U.S. withdrawal from Iraq in 2011, together with the rise of a pro-Iranian government in that Shia majority country, provided Iran with a clear route to oil-rich Kuwait and Saudi Arabia, whose large Shia minorities were restive. Bahrain was wracked by Shia upheaval, and Shia rebels in Yemen, backed by Iran, waged a guerrilla war against the country's weak government. Moreover, Israel became all but encircled militarily. The chaos in Egypt led to lawlessness in the Sinai, which soon led Hamas to take effective control along with other Islamist groups. Hamas and Fatah formed a Palestinian unity government, while Hezbollah effectively took control of Lebanon. Jordan, with its large Palestinian population, had great difficulty keeping control of its border with the West Bank.

Nor was the Middle East the only area of tension. North Korea's abrogation of the 1953 armistice agreement, together with its bellicose actions (including development of long-range ballistic missiles with WMD warheads), made East Asia increasingly unstable. In Latin America, the pro-Iranian regime in Venezuela established an anti-American alliance with such countries as Bolivia and Ecuador. Iran's alliance with North Korea, together with its establishment of a naval base on Syria's Mediterranean coast, a missile base in Venezuela and the presence of both its Revolutionary Guards and Hezbollah in Latin America (including Mexico) gave Teheran a global military reach.

All of these factors played a role in Iran's decision to initiate what would become a global struggle between the West and what would come to be known as the Red-Green Axis--Communist North Korea and the Venezuelan-led leftist bloc in Latin America, together with Iran and its proxies. Indeed, by 2015, both danger and opportunity faced the Mullahs in Teheran. Economic sanctions by Western nations resulting from Iran's nuclear program were biting deep, causing widespread disaffection and even unrest in the country. In Syria, however, the civil war had swung in favor of Iran's ally Bashar al-Assad (whose armed forces were effectively under Iranian command, with the loose coalition of rebels, including al-Qaeda groups, often fighting each other rather than Assad's forces and being driven from key areas. Thus the opportunity, created by the "Arab Spring," Israel's declining and Iran's improved strategic position, together with tensions elsewhere, gave Iran a window of opportunity to strike.

There were also the great powers, Russia and China, that had warm relations with Teheran and its allies. Both saw the American-led international order as thwarting their global ambitions, and had provided considerable support--including military aid--to the Red-Green Axis. Both had also become more bellicose in recent years. Russia had intervened militarily in Georgia, and then seized Crimea from Ukraine, while stirring up trouble in that country. China had used its growing military strength, particularly its power projection capabilities, to occupy strategic areas in the South China Sea, especially in the Spratly Islands, which it saw as being in its historic sphere of influence. Both China and Russia had expanded their presence in the Middle East and Latin America, with the express purpose of undermining the United States and establishing a new international order favorable to their interests.

A further, and perhaps more important reason for the timing of the war's outbreak was the perception of American weakness. The withdrawal from Iraq in 2011, without an adequate Status of Forces Agreement, together with the Obama Administration's mixed signals and policies toward the Middle East, created the view that the United States would not have the will to fight in defense of its allies and interests. Perhaps most importantly, the perception of declining U.S. military capacity played a key role in the thinking of the men in Teheran, Pyongyang and Caracas, and their decision to go to war. The Obama Administration's reductions in defense spending had cut some $80 billion between 2012 and 2014, as part of an overall $487 billion reduction. There were tens of thousands fewer soldiers, sailors, airmen and Marines in 2015 than there were just the year before, who would be fighting on three fronts as well as at home, and they had many fewer tanks, armored vehicles, ships and aircraft as well. Alone, any of America's enemies could be successfully defeated, along with a weaker power (Venezuela, for example.) In combination, however, it would prove to be much more difficult. Because the Iranian-led axis had the initiative, it would be able to strike heavy blows in the war's first days, further reducing U.S. combat power.

The Iranian plan was two-fold. First, to launch a full-scale attack on Israel. The first day of hostilities saw large-scale attacks by Iranian and Syrian ballistic missiles against both military and civilian targets, coordinated with rocket bombardments, guerilla assaults and terrorist attacks by Hezbollah, Hamas, and other Islamist groups deep in Israeli territory.
On the third day of hostilities, the second phase of the Iranian plan was initiated. Iranian forces made a combined amphibious and air assault on the tip of the Strait of Hormuz, in northwestern Oman. This action combined with mining and the deployment of naval and air units and missile batteries on islands at the mouth of the Strait to effectively seal it off. Iranian merchant ships and midget submarines simultaneously mined the Strait of Bab el-Mandeb and the Saudi Red Sea ports. Thus, in a day, Iran closed both the Persian Gulf and the Red Sea to Western shipping. Meanwhile, Iranian forces, which had begun to secretly move into southern Iraq, launched an invasion of Kuwait and Saudi Arabia, spearheaded by Shia uprisings, terrorist and insurgent attacks. Waves of Iranian ballistic missiles were fired against targets throughout the Gulf (including the U.S. 5th Fleet headquarters in Bahrain), while U.S. and Western naval forces in the Gulf came under attack by Iranian warships, missiles and aircraft. In the Arabian Sea, U.S. carrier groups were attacked by Iranian submarines and strike aircraft. Given the element of surprise, the Iranians inflicted considerable losses. In Afghanistan, Iran, together with al-Qaeda, launched guerilla attacks on the nearly 80,000 U.S. and ISAF troops in the country, while the Taliban launched major offensives in the east. This led to an effective siege of a large

Western force, putting great strain on airlift assets that would be needed elsewhere in the rapidly widening conflict.

Within a week, the war spread from the Middle East. North Korea, after months of bellicose rhetoric and border incidents, launched a full-scale invasion of South Korea, while making ballistic missile strikes against Japan, Guam, Hawaii and Alaska. Venezuela launched military incursions into Colombia, and soon its navy and air force were clashing with American forces in the Caribbean. Worse, from the first day of hostilities, Islamist terrorists launched mass attacks in North America, Europe and Australasia, causing mass casualties and social disruption. Large-scale cyber attacks were carried out against U.S. and Allied computer networks, both military and civilian, which played havoc with the West's infrastructure and added to the disruption caused by the terror attacks. Hezbollah guerillas crossed the Mexican border, launching attacks in the American Southwest, requiring U.S. forces to be held back from overseas deployment to combat these incursions. Within days, Iranian missiles had been launched from Venezuela against Puerto Rico, the U.S. Virgin Islands and the Caribbean territories of other NATO states, necessitating the diversion of overstretched U.S. forces to defeat this threat.

While all of this was happening, America's rival great powers made moves of their own. As unrest swept Ukraine, Russian forces, over 50,000 strong, invaded the east of that country in order to support Russian separatists, leading to large-scale fighting. China, after provoking several incidents with its neighbors in the South China Sea and deploying large naval forces there, initiated amphibious landings in several of the Spratly Islands, leading to combat with the forces of other Asian powers. Given that U.S. forces were involved in two major wars and in the Caribbean, neither the United States nor its allies were able to react effectively to these moves.

Caught largely by surprise, the United States now faced a global struggle on multiple fronts. Because its allies were either fighting for survival (Israel, South Korea) or lacked the power projection capabilities to bring sufficient forces to bear (NATO, Australia, New Zealand), most of the burden for the West's war effort fell on the U.S. military. Given their heavy early losses, U.S. forces would now have to reverse the gains of the Iranian-led axis while supporting key allies and protecting the homeland from a variety of threats. The Navy had less than 300 ships to establish sea control in the far-flung battlefronts, with fewer than 10 carriers and 30 amphibious vessels. The Air Force would have to gain air superiority with, among other aircraft, 30-year old F-15s, and its 25-year old B-1 and B-2 bombers (not to mention its 50-year old B-52s) would be pushed to their operational limits. The Marines, whose combat troops were being reduced by 13 percent, would fight from the Caribbean to the Persian Gulf to Korea with equipment whose design was in some cases 30-40 years old, while the Army, little over half a million strong, would have to wage a worldwide war. Transportation assets were taxed to the breaking point, given that many ships, planes, and even rail cars were not immediately ready for use, making it difficult to move U.S. combat forces into battle zones.

Thus, at the time of this writing, the outcome of this latest struggle between the forces of freedom and tyranny remains in doubt.

The above is of course a hypothetical scenario. However, it is well within the realm of possibility that such a conflict could occur within the near future. Most of what is stated has already taken place, and those that have not (such as a Palestinian unity government) are hardly unthinkable. Indeed, if such wild cards as missiles fitted with WMD or electromagnetic pulse (EMP) warheads are added (especially those fired from Venezuela), the results could be cataclysmic, and far sooner than the month's events described.

As this report will show, the decline of U.S. military strength, willingly engaged in by the Obama Administration, makes such a conflict far more likely to occur. When an established international order is challenged by revanchist states, and when the state that has maintained that order shows itself unable or unwilling to preserve it, then war becomes a distinct possibility. The two world wars of the last century, especially the Second, are harsh reminders of this. Only by maintaining the necessary military might to deter all enemies will the United States prevent such a conflict from occurring. It is hoped that this report will help in this effort.

Introduction--The Purposes of U.S. Military Power.

The United States is faced with a unique responsibility: the maintenance of a liberal international order, based on a system of democratic states linked by collective security and free trade. This was taken up in the years following World War II, as Britain, which had maintained a similar system since the early 19th Century, dismantled its empire and withdrew from its global role. Indeed, the two world wars of the 20th Century accelerated the abandonment of isolationism in American foreign policy and the embracing of an active international role. In both cases, the United States was compelled to fight in order to preserve the international order that Britain and its allies were unable to protect. With the onset of the Cold War and the threat of Soviet power, the United States used its military might to secure this international system. Its nuclear forces deterred those of the Soviets, while its conventional forces came to play an important role in regions of importance. In Europe, the Army and Air Force represented a concrete commitment to NATO's security, as well as in Japan and South Korea. The Navy, together with the Marines, maintained forward deployed fleets in the Mediterranean and Western Pacific as well as in the Atlantic to support U.S. allies. This posture came to include the Middle East, due to increased Soviet influence and the ever greater importance of Persian Gulf oil. The U.S. Central Command, for example, was established in 1983, at the height of the Cold War, and evolved from the Rapid Deployment Force set up in 1979-80. This included forces from all the armed services, which would combine in the event of crisis and deploy to the Gulf to counter threats to the region. America's allies in NATO, as well as in Japan, South Korea and elsewhere, were able to provide regional forces to deter the Soviet Union and its proxies, while the United States provided a military force with global reach that could deploy necessary power where needed.

The end of the Cold War saw the continuation of this policy, albeit with a different emphasis. With the collapse of the Soviet Union, the main threat to the international system--in which political and economic freedom had expanded considerably--came from revanchist states like Iraq, North Korea and Iran, as well as within failed states like Somalia and Yugoslavia. The post-Cold War era, from 1991 to 2001, saw the reversal of Iraq's invasion of Kuwait and the stabilization of the Balkans through U.S.-led NATO interventions. U.S. military planning emphasized the containment of both Iran and Iraq through an "over-the-horizon" policy in the Persian Gulf, whereby relatively small numbers of deployed U.S. forces would be reinforced in times of crisis. The containment of North Korea continued, while rapidly deployable U.S. forces (some based in NATO Europe) engaged in combat operations and peacekeeping in the Balkans.

Since 9/11, the West has found itself in a new global struggle with Islamism, together with leftist states like North Korea and Venezuela that are allied with Islamist states like Iran. The eradication of the Taliban regime in Afghanistan in 2001-02, along with the toppling of Saddam Hussein in Iraq in 2003, were the first military responses of this new conflict. The protracted wars that have been waged over the past decade have shifted the emphasis on U.S. planning toward counterinsurgency, as well as for regional wars with Iran and North Korea. Refinements of nuclear weaponry have allowed for the development of low-yield "bunker-buster" bombs to allow for strikes against hardened, underground WMD facilities.

Throughout the period since 1945, key elements have existed regarding U.S. defense policy. First has been deterrence, both nuclear and conventional. The resolution of numerous Cold War crises, most notably the Cuban Missile Crisis of 1962 and the U.S.-Soviet confrontation during the 1973 Arab-Israeli War, rested on the ability of the United States to bring to bear a preponderance of military power (including at the point of crisis) to force de-escalation by the Soviets. In 1958, the deployment of U.S. forces in Lebanon (in coordination with British forces in Jordan) prevented pro-Soviet Arab nationalist forces from gaining control of key states in an area of vital interest. Likewise, the deployment of U.S. naval forces off Taiwan in 1958 and in the Eastern Mediterranean in 1970 helped to resolve potential crises, allowing pro-Western local forces to defeat Soviet allies by providing the means to prevent escalation into wider conflicts.

A second important result of U.S. policy has been the relationship of America's military might and those of its allies. Because of the ability of the United States to project power globally, this enabled allied states to concentrate on regional defense as part of an American-led security system. This, along with democratization, has prevented traditional regional great powers (such as Germany and Japan) from building excessive military strength to deter such powers as Russia and China in the absence of American leadership. War-ravaged Western Europe and Japan were thus rebuilt to become, along with the United States, the centers of the global economy. U.S. forces were able to fill the gaps in conventional defense in NATO Europe, Japan and South Korea. This capability also allowed for U.S. forces to intervene in areas that were outside the area of responsibility of these alliances (i.e. the Persian Gulf), as well as to support allies that were politically too sensitive for action by established alliances (such as Israel.)

Today, the relationship between America's military superiority and the international system remains central. It has become even more important over the past dozen years as challenges from revanchist states and transnational actors (like al-Qaeda) have increased exponentially. The global alliance between Iran, North Korea and Venezuela (along with like-minded Latin American states) represents a bloc of revanchist states determined to overthrow the existing global structure and replace it with new orders based on radical theological and ideological views. Their increasing military potential, together with their ability to act in conjunction with guerilla and terrorist groups, makes them a growing danger for the West and its allies. Nor are these the only dangers facing the United States. The growing assertiveness of Russia and China, expressed through increasingly bellicose acts (including the supply of sophisticated weaponry to anti-Western states) and through their growing nuclear and power projection capabilities, means that a return to traditional great power confrontation, not seen since the end of the Cold War, could be in the offing.

This state of affairs has been exacerbated by the Obama Administration, whose massive sequestration cuts--some $487 billion over the next decade--have already begun to have a serious impact on U.S. military readiness and force posture. The reductions in personnel strength, especially those of the Army and Marine Corps, the fall in the number of Navy ships and especially the Air Force's inventory of tactical combat aircraft, are just some of the results of these reductions. Cancellations and delays of weapons programs vital for modernization of the services have likewise led to a situation whereby the military will have to make due with equipment that is ageing and becoming increasingly unsafe. These policies, and their effects on the different branches of the armed forces, will be the subject of the next two chapters.

Chapter 1--The Obama Administration and the Military.

Central to understanding President Obama's views on the role of the U.S. military are, of course, his views on America's role in the world. To a considerable extent, Obama's worldview differs greatly from that held by his predecessors from Harry Truman to George W. Bush. Whereas these presidents saw the United States as a defender of freedom and a bulwark against tyranny--first that of the Soviet Union, then against revanchist states and retrograde forces--Obama believes that America has had a checkered history, behaving as a colonial or even oppressive power in pursuit of imperial interests. This began to become apparent as early as 2009, when Victor Davis Hanson noted how both Obama's attempt to distance himself from his immediate predecessor and his broader view coalesced:

"In his first year in office...the president has sought to change the United States' role in the world from defender of the post-Cold War international order to apologist for its own misdeeds and agent of global change...The lynchpin of Obama's foreign policy is the assumption that America is often disliked in the world today, not primarily because of intractable problems of long ancestry, but because of the aggressive nationalism of George W. Bush during the past eight years. 'All too often,' the president assured Arab journalists, 'the United States starts by dictating.'"[i]

With this in mind, Obama sought to shape a foreign policy whereby America's enemies would not be confronted but appeased. With Iran, negotiations, rather than pressure, was to be the preferred approach regarding its nuclear program, despite the bloody crackdown by the regime on protests in June 2009. Sanctions on Syria were eased early in Obama's presidency, and an ambassador was sent to Damascus in June 2009, reversing the Bush Administration's recall in February 2005, made due to Syria's role in the murder of Lebanese prime minister Rafik Hariri.[ii] Major efforts were made to advance the establishment of a Palestinian state, including military training for Fatah,[iii] while Israel's Netanyahu was very publicly snubbed by Obama. A "reset" to Russia was made, due to what Obama believed was a hostile relationship inherited from Bush. Significantly this included the cancellation of the long-planned missile defense system in Poland, meant to protect NATO Europe from Iranian ballistic missiles. Venezuela's Hugo Chavez was also warmly treated by Obama, who supported Manuel Zelaya, a Chavez ally, in the constitutional crisis in Honduras in 2009.[iv]

It also affected the two major wars in which the United States was engaged in at the time, Iraq and Afghanistan. Obama had termed the former a "bad," that is unnecessary, war, and the latter "good" or necessary. This accounted for his divergent policies toward the two conflicts. The Status of Forces Agreement (SOFA), signed between the Bush Administration and Iraq's government in 2008, would see all U.S. forces withdrawn from the country by December 2011. In that year, efforts were made to renegotiate SOFA to allow the presence of 10-12,000 U.S. troops beyond the deadline. However, Iraqi Prime Minister Nouri al-Maliki strongly opposed this move, despite worries about security following an American withdrawal. As a result, just 5,000 private contractors, hired by the U.S. Embassy, remained after December 2011. Given Obama's opposition to the Iraq War early on (especially in his famous speech in 2002), little effort was made to press for changes to SOFA, meaning that Iran's influence was strengthened as a result of the vacuum left by the American withdrawal.

In Afghanistan, Obama decided to conduct a surge of U.S. forces, akin to that carried out by Bush in Iraq in 2007 (which was opposed by then-Senator Obama.) However, given the different circumstances, this approach--done more for public relations value than a sincere attempt to achieve victory--has not succeeded in defeating the Taliban. Indeed, the announcement that U.S. forces would withdraw by December 2014, meant that the Taliban could hunker down and await U.S. withdrawal before moving to take over much, if not all, of the country. Attempts to negotiate with so-called "moderate" Taliban elements have not achieved much either.

In other words, Obama's conduct as Commander-in-Chief was contradictory and largely ineffective, becoming more pronounced as U.S. casualties in Afghanistan grew considerably.

Early on, Obama's worldview began to shape his views on defense policy. Most important were the reductions in the defense budget. Writing in *Newsweek* on May 15, 2010, Jonathan Alter quoted Obama's view on defense spending. "For the past eight years, whatever the military asked for they got. My job was to slow things down."[v] In the summer of 2010, then Secretary of Defense Robert Gates called for $100 billion in cuts, meant to head off the deeper reductions believed to be coming. However, this was a mere stopgap measure. In spring 2011, the Defense Department was directed to prepare for cuts of up to $400 billion over the next decade, which grew to $450 billion a year later. It did not take long for this to take shape. From the last Bush budget in Fiscal Year (FY) 2010, which totaled $695.6 billion, Obama's budget for FY 2012 (after a spurt to $712.6 billion in FY 2011), fell to $650.4 billion, then to $600.4 billion in FY 2013.[vi] The FY 2014 budget stands at $496 billion.[vii] Indeed, even without the sequestration cuts of $487 billion, planned cuts since 2010 over a decade come to some $965 billion.[viii]

The FY 2015 budget is even more stark. In February 2014, Secretary of Defense Chuck Hagel proposed a budget for FY 2015 that would come to just $496 billion, itself $45 billion below President Obama's request in April 2013. Under these plans, defense spending, as a percentage of U.S. gross domestic product (GDP), would stand at 2.8 percent, comparable to pre-9/11 levels and down from 4.4 percent in 2013.[ix]

In February 2014, Secretary Hagel announced that, as part of major reductions in the FY 2015 budget, both pay and benefits for active-duty and retired personnel would be cut significantly. Pay raises for most personnel would be limited to one percent. Base commissaries in the United States would, with the exception of those in remote areas, be closed, meaning that both active personnel and retirees would face higher prices for food and health care. On-base housing expenses, which are currently fully covered, would be reduced by some five percent, forcing service members, at a time of economic difficulty, to shoulder the burden for housing. According to Norb Ryan, president of the Military Officers Association of America, these proposals for the FY 2015 budget, which include a two-year pay cap as well as the cuts in housing, mean that an Army sergeant with 10 years' service and a family of four would lose some $1,400 a year, and an Army captain would lose $2,100 by the end of FY 2015. [x] Indeed, with the fiscal uncertainty in Washington, further cuts in benefits, medical care and pay might well be in the offing, making it more difficult to attract and retain military personnel.

There has also been a marked lack of enthusiasm about protecting U.S. military personnel, both at home and abroad. The Fort Hood massacre on November 5, 2009 is a case in point. Obama refused to identify the incident as a terrorist act, and its perpetrator, Major Nidal Malik Hasan, as being inspired by radical Islam. The designation of "workplace violence" for the massacre, in the face of Hasan's fundamentalist Islamic views and his self-identification as a jihadi, is an effort to completely expunge any reference to Islamism as the guiding ideology of the United States' most dangerous and uncompromising enemies.[xi] Moreover, this designation means that those killed and wounded at Fort Hood are not eligible for the Purple Heart, since it is only awarded to those who have been wounded as a result of enemy action. This is indeed a slap in the face of those who lost life and limb in this murderous attack.

Soon after, three Navy SEALs faced court-martial for their injuring, during capture, terrorist Ahmed Hashim Abed, responsible for the bloody killing of Americans in Fallujah in 2004.[xii] As the rules of engagement in Afghanistan have shown, U.S. troops are at risk of prosecution for their actions in combat, something that has a deleterious effect on morale. The forced retirement of skilled commanders like General Stanley McChrystal, who contributed considerably to developing an effective surge strategy for Afghanistan, has also helped to undermine high-level strategic development. Thanks to the Obama Administration's attitude, it will be harder to attract Americans to serve in the military, and cause many capable career personnel to leave the service due to a feeling of indifference and even hostility from their civilian superiors. due to their actions.[xiii]

The effects of these policies began to bear bitter fruit in President Obama's second term. In August 2013, Syria's Bashar Assad used chemical weapons against civilians, killing as many as 1,400, including more than 400 children. Obama, who had declared that the use of such weapons constituted a "red line" that would lead to U.S. military action, announced that limited strikes would be carried out in response. However, the President backed away from this threat, deciding instead to accept a proposal by Assad's ally Russia for the destruction of Syria's chemical arsenal.[xiv] This has of course, led to the destruction of a small fraction of these weapons, while exposing dramatically the absence of credibility in Obama's foreign policy, especially when it comes to the use of force. This had an effect on the next major foreign policy crisis faced by the United States. In February and March 2014, Russian special forces entered and occupied the Crimea, taking control from Ukraine. While a U.S.-led military response was highly unlikely, the response of President Obama--blustering and placing gradual sanctions on Russia-- aroused mere contempt in Moscow. Indeed, the continued threat of a full-scale Russian invasion of Ukraine, together with threats to Moldova and, possibly, Estonia (a NATO member), show just how little capital the current administration has in the international arena.

More broadly, the Obama Administration's view of the struggle that has occurred since 9/11 has been an effort to convince the American people that, all evidence to the contrary, they are not at war and are not likely to be. The replacement of the term "War on Terror" with "Overseas Contingency Operations" is indicative of this, since this designation can cover a whole host of deployments, from military intervention to disaster relief. U.S. involvement in Libya in 2011-12 is an example. To be sure, some of this attitude dates from the Bush Administration. The term "War on Terror" is itself politically correct, since it did not name the ideology of the United States' primary enemies, and it limited the definition to one form of warfare, when these enemies were capable of many forms of conflict. Nevertheless, the Obama Administration's belief that there is no war or danger of it represents a denial of reality. The fact is that the United States remains at war, and it is likely to face even more bloody and destructive wars in the near future. To deny this reality will lead to disaster.

Chapter 2--The Effects of Sequestration on the Services.

The most recent--and significant--round of budget cuts for the armed forces have come as a result of sequestration. This will lead to a $487 billion reduction from the Department of Defense over the next 10 years, with $259 billion over the next five years.[xv] From $721.3 billion in FY 2010, the budget in FY 2017 will be $601.3 billion, a difference of $120 billion. While the recent budget agreement has placed sequestration on hold until 2016, when they are renewed another $600 billion in cuts will be reinstated for the next decade.[xvi] In certain areas, the reductions are striking. Modernization, vital for the maintenance of the United States' military edge, has fallen from $216 billion in FY 2010 to $178.2 billion in FY 2013, or a 17 percent reduction in this area.[xvii] Overall, these reductions will see the active armed forces reduced by 13 percent and the reserves by five percent over the coming years.[xviii] Cumulatively, as historian Arthur Herman has written in *National Review,* this will lead "toward a Navy smaller than it was before World War I, an Army smaller than it was in 1940, and an Air Force that is smaller than at any time since World War II and is acquiring fewer new aircraft than it did back in 1915."[xix] The impact of these cuts will hit all of the services hard, and it is necessary to examine these by each branch.

The Army.

The Army will face major reductions in both numbers and force structure. From a peak of 570,000 in 2011, reductions in active duty personnel levels planned for in 2013 would see this fall by 72,000 to just 490,000 over the next decade--a 13 percent reduction.[xx] In February 2014, Secretary Hagel announced that this would fall further, to 440,000-450,000.[xxi] These are well below the level of 520,000 that Army Chief of Staff General Ray Odierno publicly stated was the baseline for the Army.[xxii] This could fall even further. Depending on the Sequester, the Army could bottom out at just 380,000, according to one option laid out by Secretary Hagel.[xxiii] A total of six brigade combat teams (BCT), each with over 3,500 soldiers, will be eliminated under the proposed FY 2015 budget, with just 28 such units--the Army's standard combat formation--remaining in 2019.[xxiv] Furthermore, the Army is reducing its armored forces considerably, from 16 brigades to 10. This will see 24 companies of M-1 Abrams tanks (with 14 per company) eliminated, for a total of 336 fewer tanks.[xxv] Overall, Army ground forces will be reduced by some 20 percent.[xxvi]

Equipment modernization has also been delayed. Thanks to the proposed FY 2015 budget, procurement of a new Ground Combat Vehicle has been cancelled, while plans for a new tactical vehicle to replace the Humvee, itself now 30 years old, have been slowed.[xxvii] The Army's helicopter force, which has seen considerable combat over the past dozen years, as well as intensive use in training, is badly in need of replacement. Many helicopters were designed decades ago. The CH-47 Chinook, the Army's heavy-lift helicopter, saw extensive service in Vietnam, while the UH-60 Black Hawk first saw combat 30 years ago in Grenada. However, with the sequestration, these efforts will be delayed, making the helicopter force--central to U.S. ground combat doctrine--more unreliable and even dangerous to those who fly and ride in them.[xxviii]

Worse still, the Army's transportation system is eroding. Specialized trucks and rail cars necessary to carrying tanks and armored vehicles are now wearing out due to age and wear. In 2003, the Army had some 2,000 M1000 Heavy Equipment Trailers (HETs), capable of hauling 80-ton tanks. By 2013, however, this number had fallen to 1,500, many in need of being refurbished. The 6,000 specialized rail cars bought by the Army in the late-1960s have a service life of 50 years. The 1,300 that are owned by the Department of Defense will soon be too old for use, while the 4,500 leased from private railroads have been heavily used and will soon wear out. Because of this, the Army has been forced to use stock flatbed rail cars modified for this purpose, while making do with the remaining HETs.[xxix] Given that conventional war in the Middle East and Korea remains a distinct possibility, there remains a need for U.S. armor to be moved from bases to ports, using these platforms. If this capability continues to erode, however, the ability to deploy these forces--which could make the difference between victory or defeat--will be in doubt.

Just as serious has been the effect on the Army Reserve and National Guard. The FY 2015 proposal would see the Reserve, currently at 205,000, cut to 195,000 by 2017, while the Guard would fall from 355,000 to 335,000 during the same time. However, as Hagel himself warned, "If sequestration returns in 2016, the Army National Guard would continue drawing down further, to 315,000. Army Reserves would draw down to 185,000."[xxx] As Arthur Herman states, however, "the term 'reserves' has become a misnomer.," since the reserve forces "have evolved into the full-time support and logistical backbone of our current force." According to Herman, "In 2012...the Army National Guard made up 32 percent of Army personnel, 38 percent of the Army's operating force, and 11.5 percent of the baseline budget of the entire Army. Cutting its numbers will directly affect the viability of the standing force that remains."[xxxi] Given these facts, the reductions in reserve forces will have serious consequences for the Army, whose active forces will be under even greater strain in future conflicts. Attempts to shift capabilities between active and reserve forces, such as Hagel's plan to transfer active Army Blackhawk helicopters to Guard units in exchange for Guard Apache attack helicopters, [xxxii] will only serve to weaken active formations in critical areas, while causing the reserves' capabilities to decline by shifting priorities away from combat support to non-combat roles.[xxxiii]

All of this is occurring when the budget is being drastically reduced. The Army's budget for FY 2014 has fallen by some $14 billion.[xxxiv] Training for some units, both non-deployed and Afghan-bound, has been cut back, namely conferences and seminars that are part of normal pre-deployment training.[xxxv]

The Army has been at the forefront of the wars in Afghanistan and Iraq over the last dozen years. Its personnel, not just active duty but Reserve and National Guard, have carried out multiple combat deployments, experiencing considerable strain and, especially for Reserve and Guard personnel, considerable financial hardship as well. Their equipment has also seen much wear and tear, reducing the numbers available. Given that the Army would again bear the brunt of combat in any future war (both in large-scale battle and low intensity conflict, which could occur concurrently in different areas of the world), the need for proper funding to ensure both maintenance and modernization is essential.

The Navy.

Because of its global commitments, the United States must ensure that it maintains control of the seas, both to project power in support of allies and to deter enemies, and to protect the seaborne trade routes vital to the world economy. In a March 2014 article in the *Wall Street Journal*, Steve Cohen, former director of the U.S. Naval Institute, noted that:

"Some 90% of the world's trade moves by sea. Much of that can be disrupted by attacks on a handful of choke-points readily apparent to pirates, terrorists and rogue nations: the Strait of Hormuz, the Strait of Malacca and the Suez Canal among others. The Strait of Hormuz is only 21 miles wide, yet more than one-third of the world's seaborne oil passes through it. The damage to the world's economy would be great if it or any of the others were closed."[xxxvi]

It is essential, therefore, that the Navy be maintained as a force capable of deterring, and if necessary, defeating any enemy that challenges it. The sequestration, however, together with the Obama Administration's overall defense cuts, leave this increasingly in doubt.

The current strength of the U.S. Navy is 284 ships.[xxxvii] Of these, more than half are at sea. In 2012, 145 ships were underway at any given time. Of these, 120 were forward deployed.[xxxviii] These figures show the high tempo of operations that the Navy has been experiencing. With so few ships having to do so much, there has been much greater stress on the fleet. The budget cuts already in force have caused this situation to become even worse. The carrier fleet is a case in point. The Navy currently has 10 carriers, which are central to American naval power. This means that the carriers are continually forward deployed for months, in both peacetime and combat situations (as in support of forces in Afghanistan,) and undergo an exacting schedule. However, due to budget cuts, maintenance is becoming an increasing problem. The *Abraham Lincoln*, for example, was due to begin a four-year nuclear refueling and overhaul in February 2013. However, due to uncertainty over sequestration, this was delayed for an unspecified amount of time. At the time, the Navy was short $1.5 billion on its accounts, which grew with sequestration in March to $9 billion for the FY 2013 budget. Given that the *Lincoln*'s overhaul would cost $.3.3 billion, the funds simply were not available. As Navy spokesperson Lt. Courtney Hilllson stated, "Cancelling and deferring maintenance creates a significant backlog of deferred maintenance and affects future year schedules and cost, as well as future readiness."[xxxix]

At the same time, the deployment of the *Lincoln*'s sister ship, the *Harry S. Truman*, was delayed due to budget cuts. What made this deployment so important was that the *Truman* and her strike group were to have deployed to the Persian Gulf, at a time when confrontation over Iran's nuclear program is heating up, leaving just one carrier group on station in that vital body of water. This meant that, at least for part of 2013, there were no carriers on station in the Gulf.[xl] Nor was this the only deployment to be so affected. The Navy was forced to cancel scheduled deployments of a guided-missile destroyer, two guided-missile frigates and an attack submarine, among other ships. Additionally, four carrier air wings have been grounded and the flying time of two others restricted.[xli] Given that the Navy has just 10 carrier wings, this represents 60 percent of carrier-based naval aviation.

These problems continue. In March 2014, Admiral Jonathan Greenert, Chief of Naval Operations, had to pull $796 million in line-item funding from a list for the FY 2015 budget that would cover unfunded priorities, which would have allowed for the fuelling of the carrier *George Washington*. Instead, this will rest upon whether or not sequestration returns in 2016, which could see the *Washington*'s overhaul cancelled and the carrier--commissioned in 1992 and which the Navy would like to keep in service for another 25 years--retired from active service. This would mean that the carrier fleet would fall to 10 from 11.[xlii]

In order to compensate for the lack of new funds for maintenance, the Navy has had to use money for procurement of new ships in order to keep existing ships operational, meaning that fewer new vessels join the fleet. Moreover, because the money for maintenance is falling, this policy will lead to fewer and older ships having to serve longer and with greater wear and tear.[xliii]

As for procurement, the Navy is facing a serious problem. Naval shipbuilding for FY 2013 set a goal of 10 ships, falling to seven in FY 2014. Not until FY 2018, when 11 ships are planned, will the number of ships exceed the FY 2013 level.[xliv] The FY 2013 budget called for just 41 ships to be built over the next five years, and it will only be in 2018 that shipbuilding will be funded above replacement levels--that is, increasing the number of ships in service. Under the FY 2013 budget, nine ships were retired, reducing an already small fleet and complicating plans for even limited naval increases.[xlv] In January 2013, the Navy was forced to scale down its already modest goal of 313 ships--made in 2005--to just 306 ships.[xlvi] Events since then have put this figure into doubt. The proposed FY 2015 budget would see $15 billion cut from the Navy's funds, leading to additional reductions in force levels and procurement.[xlvii] According to the Congressional Budget Office, taking into account both shipbuilding and retirement for the period from 2014 to 2043, the Navy will not reach its 306-ship goal until 2037.[xlviii]

In an April 2012 op-ed in the *Wall Street Journal*, John Lehman, Secretary of the Navy in the Reagan Administration, warned that, even at a shipbuilding rate of eight ships per year, the Navy would fall to 240-250 ships "at best," given the concurrent retirement of vessels already in service.[xlix] This was well below the recommendation made in the Quadrennial Defense Review Independent Panel, led by Stephen Hadley and William Perry (Secretary of Defense in the Clinton Administration) in 2011, which recommended a baseline 346-ship force for the Navy.[l] In March 2014, Admiral Greenert told the House Armed Services Committee that "For us to meet what combatant commanders request" that is, to carry out the Navy's global responsibilities, "we need a Navy of 450 ships."[li]

There is also a shortfall in the number of ships being built and those remaining in service. Only one large-deck amphibious ship will be built in FY 2017, with only three more amphibious vessels being built by FY 2022.[lii] There are currently 30 amphibious ships in service, down from 36 in 2005.[liii] While the carrier force stands at 11 ships, this will probably fall to 10 as a result of the retirement of the *Washington*.[liv] The *Gerald R. Ford*, lead ship of a new carrier class, will not enter service until 2016.[lv] Under plans put forward by Secretary Hagel as a result of Sequestration, the carrier fleet could be reduced by two ships.[lvi] Procurement of the Littoral Combat Ship (LCS), vital for use in confined waters like the Persian Gulf, has been cut back from 52 ships to 32,[lvii] while plans for a 55-boat force of attack submarines could be in jeopardy.[lviii] Lehman noted that, "in order to pay for current operations, Mr. Obama is retiring 11 modern combat ships (seven cruisers and four amphibious vessels) well before their useful life."[lix] As a result of the FY 2015 budget, half of the Navy's cruiser force--11 ships in all--will be removed from service or placed on reduced operating status while being modified.[lx] Another six ships would be mothballed in 2016, while the procurement of destroyers would be slowed.[lxi]

Nor is shipbuilding the only area of procurement that the Navy is having difficulties with. A total of 49 F-35C Joint Strike Fighters, designed for use from carrier decks, were to be procured between 2015 and 2018. As a result of budget cuts, this number will be just 20.[lxii] The P-8A Poseidon patrol aircraft will also face reductions, with just 49 aircraft to be delivered over this same period, rather than the 56 originally planned for.[lxiii] Missile procurement has also fallen, with the Hellfire laser-guided air-to-ground missile to be cancelled and the Joint Standoff Weapon (JSOW-C) to be reduced by more than 75 percent during this same period.[lxiv]

Most seriously, the Tomahawk cruise missile, the primary long-range strike weapon of the U.S. Navy, will have it's production run ended. For FY 2015, plans called for some 980 of these missiles to be procured. The revised budget allows for just 100, with none to be added after.[lxv] This decision will have dire consequences not only for the Navy, but for overall U.S. military capabilities. The Tomahawk, in its Block IV variant, is a peerless weapon, equipped with a jam-resistant GPS receiver and a two-way satellite data-link that allows these missiles to be re-routed in flight.[lxvi] Deployed on cruisers, destroyers and submarines (including submarines of Britain's Royal Navy), it allows for prompt, precision strikes against heavily-defended targets, a capability that has been vital for the success of U.S. and Allied forces for more than 20 years. Given that a successor to Tomahawk will not come on line until the 2020s, this decision, if approved, will leave a dangerous gap in U.S. long-range strike capabilities, at a time when the need for such capabilities is increasing.

These reductions in funding and procurement have severely affected the Navy's ability to carry out its global responsibilities. In an April 7, 2014 speech at the Navy League's annual Sea-Air-Space expo outside Washington, D.C., Admiral Greenert noted that "We have a covenant to provide three carrier strike groups and three amphibious ready groups in a crisis. And if we go back to sequestration, we'll be at one. And, by the way, right now we're at one. We're still recovering from this period of fiscal uncertainty."[lxvii] Speaking at the same venue, Admiral William Gortney, head of the Navy's Fleet Forces Command, noted the difficulties in getting back to an eight-month deployment schedule for carrier strike groups, down from the usual 10 months in recent years. "Eight months is right on the ragged edge of what's acceptable."[lxviii] Beginning in 2015, there will be a 50 percent reduction in the number of carriers deployed on station, while only a quarter of the Navy's ships will be deployed, down from today's total of 81.[lxix]

The best summary of the above situation was given by Vice Admiral Thomas Copeman, commander of the U.S. Pacific Fleet's surface naval forces: "Not enough people, not enough parts, not enough training, not enough everything." He continued by noting that "[Operational] tempos have increased, resources have gone down."[lxx]

All this would be bad enough if it were done, say, in a time of what appeared to be perpetual peace, as was believed in the post-Cold War 1990s. That it is happening as the likelihood of major war increases makes this potentially catastrophic. The Middle East is becoming ever more unstable, with the Syrian civil war likely to spread, Iran's drive for nuclear weapons continuing and the "Arab Spring" still very far from playing itself out. Korea remains tense, and the growing assertiveness and military capacity of China means that the Asia-Pacific region is slowly becoming an arena of conflict. This means that naval power will be essential to support America's allies and to bring U.S. military strength to bear. However, the Navy, despite the superiority of its ships, aircraft, weapon systems and personnel, is increasingly unable to successfully carry out such a far-reaching task. A fleet of 284 ships, facing serious issues of maintenance and procurement, will be ever more hard-pressed to carry out its responsibilities, given that many of the United States' allies have reduced their far smaller navies to the point where they can provide only limited support to the U.S. Navy.

As Seth Cropsey, former Deputy Under-Secretary of the Navy in the Reagan and Bush Sr. Administrations, has warned in his new book <u>Mayday: The Decline of American Naval Supremacy</u>: "If the United States does not have the military capacity to continue a grand strategy based importantly on sea-based forces, then American grand strategy will crumble."[lxxi]

The Air Force.

Even worse off than the Navy is the Air Force. Between 2008 and 2012, the Air Force retired 700 more aircraft that it purchased.[lxxii] Already, in the dozen-plus years since 2001, it's inventory has fallen considerably, with its fighter force falling by 25 percent. Its 52 F-117 stealth fighters have been retired, along with 263 F-15s and 372 F-16s.[lxxiii] Given the ground wars in Afghanistan and Iraq and the perceived lower priority of a large force of fighter aircraft, along with the age of many of the fighters retired and limitations of some aircraft (the F-117 had no air-to-air capability, for example), this fall, while serious, did not overly affect the Air Force's capability, especially when new fighters like the F-22 Raptor began to enter service.

However, the Obama Administration's reductions in defense spending have had severe effects for the Air Force. The FY 2013 budget saw six tactical fighter squadrons plus a training squadron cut from the Air Force's order of battle,[lxxiv] while a total of 17 squadrons of combat aircraft were grounded as a result of sequestration.[lxxv] Among the units affected were a squadron each of F-22s and F-15E Strike Eagles, together with four F-16 wings plus three squadrons, two squadrons of B-1B bombers and one of B-52s, as well as two of A-10C close support aircraft, while another A-10 squadron was closed. Additionally, several other combat units have been restricted to minimal flying hours.[lxxvi] The Red Flag exercise--vital for realistic air combat training--was cancelled for the rest of the year, while delays have been made to testing and upgrading for numerous aircraft, including the F-22.[lxxvii]

Nor were combat units alone in these cuts. The FY 2013 budget would see 130 transport aircraft retired as well, mainly C-5A's, C-27s and C-130s, significantly reducing U.S. airlift potential.[lxxviii] The Air Force also faces cost overruns on its programs for space systems modernization, and the need to reconfigure its intelligence, reconnaissance and surveillance assets from counter-insurgency and anti-terror to more conventional roles.[lxxix]

Even without sequestration, the Air Force will shed $54 billion from its budget over the next five years, making not only procurement, but maintenance of the existing or even smaller force far more difficult.[lxxx] Already, the Air Force has faced considerable difficulties in procuring new aircraft as a result of Obama Administration policies. In 2009, the number of F-22 Raptor fighters was capped at 187, whereas estimates from officials and Air Force commanders called for between 243 and 381, in order to maintain an effective fighter force, especially as many of the "Legacy" fighters--F-15s and F-16s-- would be nearing the end of the their effective service lives.[lxxxi] The average age of the F-15C/D's, for example, is nearly 30 years. During a training mission in St. Louis in 2007, an F-15 broke in half, leading to the grounding of the entire force for several months.[lxxxii] All this would leave the Air Force with a fighter shortfall of 800 aircraft between 2017 and 2024.[lxxxiii]

The FY 2013 budget delayed the procurement of many joint programs that are central to the Air Force's modernization. Among these are the F-35A Joint Strike Fighter (JSF), whose procurement was seen as mitigating the capping of F-22 production, and the Joint Air-to-Ground Munition program. Whereas the Air Force planned to take delivery of 264 F-35A's by FY 2017, for example, this has been slashed to just 166.[lxxxiv] It also cancels the Global Hawk Block 30 and the Defense Weather Satellite System, both vital for the modernization of the Air Force's surveillance and space assets.[lxxxv] The KC-46A tanker, a much-needed replacement for the Air Force's ageing KC-135s and KC-10s, will also see its entry into service pushed back as a result of these cuts, which will be made worse as Sequestration kicks in.

With the FY 2015 budget, the situation has gotten much worse. The Air Force's budget has fallen to $109.3 billion, down from a proposed $114.1 billion, and could fall further in FY 2016 if Sequestration goes back into effect.[lxxxvi] The FY 2015 budget would see some 500 aircraft retired from the Air Force's inventory, both active and reserve, over the next five years. While some of the planes to be phased out, like the U-2 spyplane dating back more than 50 years, are in need of retirement (and have much more capable replacements in service), most are vital to the retention of an effective combat capability. Among these aircraft are the entire force of A-10 attack aircraft--vital for close support against both insurgents in Iraq and Afghanistan and against the armored formations of potential enemies like Iran and North Korea--and significant reductions in the force of F-15 and F-16 fighters.[lxxxvii] If 2016 does see Sequestration, another 80 aircraft would join the 500 being retired as a result of this year's budget. The KC-10 tanker force and the Global Hawk Block 40 would be retired, with significant slowing of F-35 procurement (24 fewer aircraft through FY 2019) and a 20 percent reduction in patrols by Predator and Reaper UAV's.[lxxxviii] It would also see a reduction in flying hours, adversely affecting readiness.[lxxxix]

All these reductions will have a serious effect on the Air Force's ability to wage war, particularly as Russia and China have begun to produce combat aircraft that are equivalent to the "fifth generation" combat aircraft like the F-22 and F-35 JSF. As these aircraft enter the export market, they will make their way into the inventories of America's adversaries, meaning that the likelihood of U.S. pilots seeing air-to-air combat increases. If war breaks out on several fronts, the Air Force will have to carry out its missions of air superiority, close air support and strategic strike with fewer and older aircraft. The growing age of the bomber force, not just the B-52H's (last built in 1962), but the B-1B (last built in 1988) and B-2A (2000), and the reductions in numbers, means that the ability to carry out global strike missions--a capability unique to the United States--will decline in the next few years, since a new long-range bomber will not be developed, let alone deployed, until at least 2025.[xc] Furthermore, the reductions in airlift assets will mean that the rapid deployment of U.S. forces to crisis areas or battlefronts across the globe will be diminished considerably, reducing both the deterrent capability of U.S. forces and their ability to prevail in combat.

The Marine Corps.

The U.S. Marine Corps has, with good reason, become known as "America's 911 force," due to its ability to provide on-scene combat formations at the point of crisis. The Marines' unique capability lies in their amphibious capabilities, which allows for the forward deployment of self-sustained units--usually a reinforced battalion, air group and support elements--aboard amphibious ships. These units can be deployed to respond to a crisis--an enemy incursion, an embassy attack, a humanitarian disaster, etc.--as a lead element that can be reinforced by follow-up forces. Because they are deployed at sea, in international waters and do not--with a few exceptions like Okinawa and, more recently, Australia--require foreign bases, they can deploy in various force packages (sometimes in brigade strength) without the need to gain the approval of foreign powers to use their territory that, say, overseas-based Army units might. Their self-sustainability, up to two weeks, gives the Marines the ability to diffuse many crisis situations without resort to larger forces, which also serves to deter potential opponents from threatening U.S. interests.

Given these capabilities, the Marine Corps should be exempt from any significant cuts. However, it too is facing some serious reductions over the next few years. From a current active level of 202,000, the Marine Corps will fall to 182,000--a 10 percent reduction in force.[xci] If Sequestration occurs in FY 2016, this level could go down to 175,000.[xcii]

While this does not appear at first to be as significant as, say, the reductions in Army strength, it is in the types of units that will be reduced that problems occur. The overall number of combat troops is being reduced by 13 percent. This translates to an 11 percent reduction in infantry, 20 percent in armor and 20 percent in artillery. The number of infantry battalions--which are the backbone of forward deployed Marine Expeditionary Units (MEU) that provide the spear tip of Marine forces--will fall from 27 to 24.[xciii]

Worse still has been the effect on retention of officers and NCOs, many with invaluable combat experience. Marine sergeants needed to be promoted before their 13th year of service or face retirement. With the need to reduce its ranks, the Marine Corps has reduced this to 10 years. This will mean that hundreds of veteran NCOs will be forced out. Similarly, officers with less than 20 years' service are being offered early retirement, which will have a similar effect on the officer corps.[xciv] Some areas are being expanded, like cyber warfare, special operations and support units, while at least three law enforcement support battalions will be created.[xcv] However, the reduction of combat units and the loss of experienced leaders will have a negative impact on the Marines' overall combat capability. Ironically, these reductions come as the Corps has just increased to Congressionally-mandated levels (from 180,000). While the Marine Reserve will remain at its current strength (39,600), it will face greater responsibility in support of active units, without being augmented by officers and NCOs retired from active service whose experience would be useful.[xcvi]

In equipment, too, the Marine Corps is facing serious difficulties, especially with modernization. The standard amphibious assault vehicle is the AAV-7, 1,300 of which are in service as troop carriers, repair vehicles and command-and-control vehicles.[xcvii] While these have served the Marines well in several conflicts, including Iraq and Afghanistan, the basic design is over 40 years old. Moreover, the AAV-7's have seen considerable use in combat over the past decade, and are suffering from considerable wear and tear. While funds were provided in FYs 2005 and 2006 to modernize 327 of the vehicles,[xcviii] eventually they will need to be replaced. However, this has met with considerable difficulty. The Expeditionary Fighting Vehicle, which was supposed to replace the AAV-7s beginning in FY 2008, ran into cost overruns and was cancelled in 2011. A new design, the Amphibious Combat Vehicle, was announced in 2012, but it has been cancelled under Hagel's FY 2015 budget.[xcix] Needless to say, this will have a highly negative impact on the Marines' amphibious assault and mobility capabilities.

Another area affected is Marine aviation. Thanks to budget cuts, in 2013 the F-35B vertical take-off variant of the Joint Strike Fighter, had its entry into service delayed by at least two years. This forced the Marines to extend the useful life of their AV-8B Harriers to 2030, and have been able to do so mainly by purchasing Britain's recently retired Harrier fleet.[c] This means that an aircraft that entered service in the mid-1980s will have to soldier on to the 2030s, providing close air support to Marine ground forces while contending with ever more sophisticated fighters, surface-to-air missiles and anti-aircraft artillery.

Cuts in spending have also led to a reduction in the Marines' ability to deploy to vital areas. In September 2012, Maritime Prepositioning Squadron One, stationed in the Mediterranean, was disestablished.[ci] Its five ships carried enough equipment and supplies to support a full-strength Marine Expeditionary Brigade--flown in from the United States--for 30 days. Given continued instability in the Middle East that could require the deployment of U.S. troops in several countries in response to a host of contingencies, this decision will greatly increase the difficulties faced in responding effectively. Reductions in the Navy's amphibious forces have also raised concern. On March 25, 2014, 20 former Marine generals, including James Conway, former Commandant, and James Mattis, former commander-in-chief of the U.S. Central Command, sent a signed letter to Congress calling for increased procurement of amphibious ships, warning that "The challenges of diminished ship material readiness and the declining numbers of amphibious warships are interrelated and have [a] cumulative effect on the nation's ability to support strategic imperatives." While both the Navy and Marine Corps have stated that a force of 38 amphibious ships--capable of transporting a force of two Marine Expeditionary Brigades or 30,000 men--is needed to meet combined requirements, the current goal is just 33 ships, which will not be reached until FY 2018.[cii]

Like the Army, the Marines are also having to reduce training schedules. While this has mostly affected non-deployed units, some formations bound for Afghanistan have had conferences and seminars canceled.[ciii]

All this points to difficult times for the Marine Corps, which translates to problems in U.S. national security strategy. The Marines' amphibious capabilities provide the most effective means of projecting power into hostile territory. Even in Afghanistan in 2001, a MEU was the first conventional U.S. combat unit to deploy. In the potential areas of conflict that the United States faces--the Persian Gulf, Korea, the Eastern Mediterranean and, quite possibly, the Caribbean--amphibious assault would be vital for U.S. forces, both to stem enemy advances and initiate counteroffensives. If the Marine Corps finds itself lacking the proper equipment and the necessary formations for such a mission, it will be much more difficult to successfully carry out these objectives, and much more difficult for the U.S. armed forces as a whole to prevail in such conflicts.

Chapter 3--The U.S. Nuclear Deterrent and the Wish for Disarmament.

Since coming into office in January 2009, President Obama has sought to reduce to the greatest extent possible the size of the U.S. nuclear deterrent. One of his most important foreign policy objectives was the signing of a New Strategic Arms Reduction Treaty (New START) with Russia. Completed in 2010, this would see the United States and Russia reduce their arsenals to 1,550 deployed warheads apiece. In presenting the treaty to the Senate for ratification, President Obama made two key promises. First, "to... modernize or replace the triad of strategic nuclear delivery systems: a heavy bomber and air-launched cruise missile, an ICBM [intercontinental ballistic missile], a nuclear-powered ballistic missile submarine (SSBN) and SLBM [submarine-launched ballistic missile]. Second, to "maintain the United States rocket motor industrial base."[civ] As a condition for New START ratification, Obama promised to invest $85 billion over 10 years after 2010 to improve both the U.S. arsenal and its infrastructure.[cv]

How well has the President kept his promises? If we look at the motor industrial base, rather badly. Obama had promised to provide funding to design and build the Chemistry and Metallurgy Research and Replacement (CMRR) building and the Uranium Processing Facility (UPF) necessary for maintaining the base. However, the administration recommended deferring construction of the CMRR for five years, reducing by 83 percent funding in the FY 2013 budget below what it was in FY 2012. This went against Obama's promise to preserve a critical capability at the CMRR made to the Senate as part of ratification.[cvi]

Then there was the deterrent itself. In 2012, the U.S. strategic forces fielded 488 Minuteman III ICBMs with 688 warheads, 336 Trident II D-5 SLBMs with 2,016 warheads aboard 14 SSBNs, and 56 B-52H and 15 B-2A bombers with 528 air-launched cruise missiles and bombs.[cvii] Many of these systems are long in the tooth, especially the Minuteman III's which were last procured in 1978. Six of the 14 *Ohio*-class SSBNs were commissioned before 1990, and the newest in 1997.[cviii] Warheads too are ageing. The 450 W78 warheads deployed on some 250 Minuteman IIIs and the W88s on many Trident SLBMs are urgently in need of life extension programs to maintain their utility.[cix] Some of the older bombs in the U.S. arsenal are still equipped with transistor-tubes.[cx]

However, funding for necessary modernization of the nuclear arsenal has not been forthcoming. The first phase of planned strategic modernization--which includes a new 12-boat SSBN fleet--is estimated to cost $335 billion over the next decade, according to the Congressional Budget Office, with the Center for Nonproliferation Studies estimating that the full-scale modernization program, carried out over 30 years--will cost $1 trillion.[cxi] Given the massive reductions in defense spending, the continued threat of Sequestration in 2016 and the need for conventional force maintenance and modernization, the implementation of even the initial phase of nuclear modernization remains in question. Indeed, many necessary improvements have already been affected.

The modification of W78s and W88s, a new long-range standoff cruise missile and other necessary programs have been delayed, while a new plutonium laboratory in New Mexico--urgently needed to maintain the nuclear weapons production base--has been cancelled.[cxii] According to Rep. Mike Rogers, chairman of the House Armed Services Subcommittee on Strategic Forces, the administration is underfunding the nuclear forces by some $1-1.6 billion.[cxiii]

There has also been a delay on the procurement of new SSBNs. A review of the defense budget on January 26, 2012 by then-Secretary Leon Panetta noted that the acquisition of the new submarine will be delayed.[cxiv] While the program remains, the first of these new boats will not be operational until FY 2029, and will not carry out a deterrent patrol until 2031. A U.S. Navy report to Congress in February 2010 warned that the first new SSBN "must be procured no later than FY 2019 to ensure that 12 operational ballistic missile submarines will always be available to perform the vital strategic deterrent mission."[cxv] Given the new round of defense cuts and reductions under New START, whether or not this is a realistic goal remains to be seen.[cxvi]

The reductions in warhead numbers have also strained the U.S. strategic forces. Testifying before the Senate in 2010, General Kevin Chilton, head of the U.S. Strategic Command, stated that the ceiling of 1,550 warheads stipulated by New START was the lowest acceptable number, given the need to preserve the flexibility of the U.S. strategic triad.[cxvii] Now, however, this is likely to fall even further. As part of the Nuclear Posture Review implementation study, President Obama may use executive action, without the authorization of Congress, to unilaterally reduce the U.S. warhead level to just 1,000--a one-third reduction.[cxviii] Indeed, in his June 2013 speech in Berlin, the President announced a proposal--to be carried out jointly by the United States and Russia via arms control agreements--to reduce strategic warheads to this level by 2018.[cxix] Nor could this be the last such reduction. As early as 2012, plans for defense cuts led some to believe that the Obama Administration could cut the number of warheads to just 300-400.[cxx]

Already, the New START reductions are taking effect. Each of the 14 *Ohio*-class SSBN's are having four of their 24 launch tubes modified to launch cruise missiles or satellite launchers rather than SLBMs. This will reduce the number of deployable Trident missiles to just 280. 50 Minuteman IIIs are having their warheads removed, and 30 B-52s are having their nuclear capability removed and will carry only conventional smart bombs.[cxxi]

These cuts are central to Obama's view of the United States' role in the world, which holds that the United States is responsible for the continuing presence of nuclear weapons and sees as a corrective the reduction of U.S. nuclear forces in response.[cxxii] It also holds that U.S. nuclear reductions will somehow lead to other powers making sincere efforts at disarmament in response to American initiatives. New START is a prime example of this.

Apart from the ideological view of blaming the United States, this approach flies in the face of factual reality. Both Russia and China are undertaking major improvements to their nuclear forces, while smaller powers are moving forward with development and deployment of nuclear weaponry.

Russia, for example, is now in the process of modernizing its strategic arsenal, which atrophied after the fall of the Soviet Union. In March 2013, according to a report from the Bulletin of the Atomic Scientists, Russia had 1,800 strategic warheads deployed on missiles and at bomber bases.[cxxiii] A new mobile ICBM, the Yars-M, with a range of 6,835 miles and 10 warheads, is being deployed.[cxxiv] Development of a new heavy ICBM, meant to replace 1970s-vintage SS-18s, has begun, and could enter service by 2018, giving Russia a unique offensive strategic capability.[cxxv] Additionally, a new rail-mobile ICBM will deploy by 2020, when a new strategic bomber will be also be deployed. A new air-launched cruise missile will be deployed this year, while a submarine-launched cruise missile is under development.[cxxvi] In January 2013, a new Russian SSBN, the first in over 20 years, was deployed. Two more submarines of the class are under construction.[cxxvii] A new SLBM, the Bulava "Mace," is currently being filght-tested. It is equipped with 6-10 hypersonic maneuvering nuclear warheads, designed for the purpose of penetrating U.S. missile defenses, with accuracy that allows it to destroy hardened missile silos and command centers.[cxxviii]

In tactical weapons, too, the Russians have an advantage. Under New START, Russia enjoys a considerable lead over the United States in tactical warheads, some 3,800 to fewer than 500, and has a much more flexible arsenal of weapons (including cruise missiles) than does the United States[cxxix] President Obama's proposal--made in Berlin in June 2013 in the same speech calling for cuts below New START--that the United States, working with NATO and Russia to seek "bold reductions" in European-based tactical nuclear weapons--is unlikely to have much impact, given the current state of U.S.-Russian relations, and would do little to improve the U.S. tactical force committed to NATO Europe.[cxxx]

China has also been modernizing. Three new mobile ICBMs--the DF-31, DF-31A and DF-41 are in service or under development, as is a new SLBM, the JL-2. A new class of SSBN is also being built, and it is planned that five submarines with 60 JL-2s will enter service. This will increase China's arsenal from some 240 to 420 warheads. Reports indicate that two *Jin*-class SSBNs will deploy on their first patrols in the Northern Pacific, carrying 12-16 JL-2s-with a 14,000 km. range and as many as 10 warheads---and putting both Alaska and Hawaii, along with parts of the Continental United States, within range of forward-deployed Chinese strategic forces.[cxxxi] More worrisome, the latest Chinese defense white paper made no mention of the country's previously stated "no-first-use" policy regarding nuclear weapons.[cxxxii] Pakistan is receiving assistance from China in modernizing its arsenal of missiles and warheads.[cxxxiii]

For its part, North Korea is believed to be developing missile warheads. Having conducted three underground nuclear tests, North Korea is believed to be preparing to test a "fusion-boosted-fission-bomb." This could be placed in a warhead, possibly carried by such long range missiles as the Taepodong-2 or KN-08, North Korea's new mobile ICBM.[cxxxiv] Iran, which is working on its own nuclear weapons program, receives considerable assistance from North Korea, and could have similar capabilities in the near future.

These developments exposed the folly of the Obama Administration's views on nuclear disarmament. Not only are these states increasing their nuclear capabilities, but they are becoming more hostile to the United States. China's belligerent stance toward its neighbors and its view of the United States as an adversary is one example. Russia, too is cool toward the United States, exemplified by its stance on Syria and its action against Ukraine.[cxxxv] Iran and North Korea are of course enemies, and Pakistan, wracked by political instability and growing anti-Americanism, could indeed move in this direction. As videnced by recent events in Ukraine--which eliminated its nuclear arsenal in the 1990s in return for respect of its territorial integrity--the need to maintain or acquire a nuclear arsenal in order to deter real or potential aggressors has been a lesson not lost on many states, meaning that the proliferation of nuclear-armed states--including perhaps such U.S. allies as Saudi Arabia, South Korea and even Japan--will continue, rather than contract.[cxxxvi]

Indeed, Saudi Arabia may be an example of this trend. At the end of April 2014, at the conclusion of a major military exercise, a pair of Chinese-made DF-3 intermediate-range missiles, believed to be nuclear-capable due to their lack of accuracy, were displayed in a military parade.[cxxxvii] According to experts, it is believed that Saudi Arabia has made a secret agreement with Pakistan to utilize the latter's nuclear warheads for the DF-3s in case of a conflict or crisis, namely with Iran. This follows a visit to China by Saudi defense officials, which, according to reports, may have led to the sale of DF-21 ballistic missiles--far more advanced than the DF-3's that have been in the Saudi arsenal since the 1980s. As Simon Henderson, a Washington Institute analyst on the Middle East, has written, "The missile display signals Saudi Arabia's determination to counter Tehran's growing strength, as well as its readiness to act independently of the United States...In particular, the presence of Pakistan's top military commander [at the Saudi military parade] will reawaken speculation that Riyadh may seek to acquire nuclear warheads from Islamabad to match Iran's potential."[cxxxviii] This, in turn, could lead to other Mideast states, like Egypt, Turkey and smaller Gulf nations, to obtain nuclear weapons and delivery systems for deterrence as well, destabilizing an already unstable region to an even greater degree.[cxxxix]

Given these developments, it is incumbent on the United States to maintain a balanced and flexible nuclear deterrent, large and versatile enough to deter both major powers and emerging nuclear states in support of its interests and allies. As in the Cold War, U.S. nuclear and conventional forces are mutually reinforcing. Nuclear forces can deter an enemy from using similar weaponry against U.S. conventional forces, preventing a dangerous escalation of conflict. If this fails, then selected strikes can be made that minimize damage and casualties while ensuring the elimination of the threat at hand. It is therefore of utmost necessity that the disastrous approach of the Obama Administration must be challenged and reversed. Otherwise, the use of WMD in a future conflict, which we of course seek to avoid, becomes much more likely.

Chapter 4--The Global Environment.

The Threats to America's Strategic Interests.

Being at the center of the international system, the United States faces challenges in many parts of the world. This has become increasingly so since 2001, not only because of 9/11, but a growing assertiveness among revanchist and revisionist powers and associated non-state groups. Since the Obama Administration came into office in 2009, these challenges have intensified, due in no small part to the perception of American weakness and retrenchment that the new president put forward.

The areas of interest to the United States that are most vulnerable are the Middle East, East Asia and Latin America. In each of these regions, a hostile power, often with allies, openly challenges the international system that is maintained by the United States. Moreover, these powers cooperate with one another for the same goal, and thus present a global front against American leadership.

In the Middle East, the situation has become ever more unstable since the "Arab Spring" of 2011, which unleashed unprecedented turmoil. The fall of Mubarak in Egypt and of the existing regime in Tunisia, together with the rise of a Muslim Brotherhood government and its subsequent overthrow by the Egyptian military has transformed once-solid U.S. allies into states with uncertain futures. The fall of Qaddafi's regime in Libya has resulted in al-Qaeda effectively taking control of much of the country. Shia unrest has caused upheaval in Bahrain and Yemen, while there and in Jordan the Muslim Brotherhood is leading large-scale protest movements that threaten stability. Syria's civil war has drawn in Iran and the Gulf states in support of their respective sides, and has spilled over into Lebanon and Iraq, where al-Qaeda has made a bloody resurgence. These developments have also eroded Israel's security, with Hamas in control of Gaza, Hezbollah wielding considerable power in Lebanon and the Sinai now open to Islamist groups.

The United States' main adversary in the Middle East is Iran. Its Shia revolutionary ideology sees itself as destined to "cleanse" the Middle East of American influence and to destroy Israel. Its position has become increasingly favorable over the past few years. The U.S. withdrawal from Iraq in 2011, which left little concrete American influence in the country, has led Iran to establish close ties with its prime minister, Nouri al-Maliki. The large and restive Shia populations in many Gulf states, including Saudi Arabia, also provide a means for Iran to expand its influence. Cooperation with like-minded Sunnis (such as Iran's tactical alliances with al-Qaeda and the Taliban, and its friendly relations with Egypt's new government), expand Teheran's influence further.

This presents a threat to two key U.S. interests--the survival of Israel and the security of the Persian Gulf. The encirclement of Israel by hostile forces--along with the possibility of Islamist revolution in Jordan--make it much harder for her to defend herself against a combined assault on all fronts. Iran's nuclear weapons program, coupled with the development of ballistic missiles, adds to these difficulties. In the Persian Gulf, the instability in such key U.S. allies as Bahrain and Saudi Arabia threatens oil supplies vital to global economic stability, as well as America's ability to protect them militarily. Iraq provides a gateway for Iran to use force against the Gulf states as well, and Iran's coastline along the Gulf's northern littoral, including the Strait of Hormuz, gives it the ability to stop tanker traffic. With the Syrian civil war intensifying, this could lead to a wider conflict, which could see Iran initiate hostilities to achieve its goals.

In East Asia, the most immediate threat is North Korea. Its growing nuclear capability, both in warheads and missiles, extends its threat radius, which in a few years could reach the United Sates. Its growing bellicosity, driven by its dire economic and demographic situation and its alienation even from close allies like China, could see it initiate a war to conquer the South, in the belief that it would eliminate the most dangerous threat to its existence. Such a conflict would exact an enormous cost, and have severe repercussions throughout the world.

As for Latin America, the anti-American bloc led by Venezuela--which includes Bolivia, Ecuador, Nicaragua and, most recently, El Salvador--is challenging U.S. leadership, which had been secure there since the end of the Cold War. Nicolas Maduro, Hugo Chavez' successor as president, has continued the anti-American policies of his predecessor. Moreover, Venezuela is undertaking a major military buildup with Russian weapons. Its support for Colombia's FARC guerrillas and its alliance with Iran, which has led to a substantial Hezbollah presence in the country, are examples of its efforts to undermine the U.S. position.[cxl] In November 2010, Iran and Venezuela signed an agreement to establish a jointly-manned missile base in Venezuela. Caracas reportedly gave Teheran permission to use these missiles in an "emergency." Depending on the weapons deployed, this could put the United States itself in danger of an Iranian military strike.[cxli]

There are also the great powers, Russia and China, which have also taken an increasingly adversarial stance toward the United States. Under Vladimir Putin, Russia has begun to restore its international status, rebuilding its military and supporting allies like Iran, Syria and Venezuela with arms supplies and even (Syria) military deployments. Russia's actions in the Crimea have increased tensions with the West, with the possibility of military conflict with the Ukraine as a result of Russian incursions into the east of that country. This has also impacted efforts to prevent Iran from achieving nuclear weapons capability. Russia is unlikely to support resuming sanctions on Teheran if negotiations fall through, narrowing the time frame for Iran deploy nuclear weapons as well as increasing the possibility that Israel might strike at Iran's nuclear facilities, with all attendant risks, as a result.[cxlii]

China has also been increasing its military strength, establishing a power projection capability in the South China Sea in support of its claims to the resource-rich Spratly Islands, and has provoked border disputes with India (with which it fought a war in 1962 and whose arch-enemy, Pakistan, is a Chinese ally). China's efforts to take control of islands from the Philippines, to drill in waters claimed by Vietnam and its claims on the Senkaku Islands, under Japanese control, have seen Chinese naval and coast guard vessels used aggressively to assert Chinese rights and to intimidate what Beijing sees as its adversaries.

Both Russia and China view themselves as regional great powers--Russia in Eastern Europe and the Balkans, China in East Asia. Both also believe that the dominant position enjoyed by the United States since 1991 is an inhibitor to these goals, and see an opportunity, provided by Barrack Obama, to weaken or even supplant America's unipolar position with a multipolar order in which Moscow and Beijing would be key players.

Capabilities of America's Adversaries.

Both America's direct enemies (Iran, North Korea and Venezuela) and its great power rivals (Russia and China) field considerable military capabilities. In the first category must also be included non-state actors, namely guerilla and terrorist groups that are supported by or allied to these states.

Iran: Central to the anti-American "Red-Green Axis", Iran fields large and diverse forces that present a significant threat. In mid-2012, Iran's armed forces fielded 520,000 men. Of these, 398,000 were in the regular armed forces (350,000 in the army, 18,000 each in the navy and air force, and 12,000 in the air defense force), with another 100,000 in the Iranian Revolutionary Guards Corps (IRGC) ground force and 20,000 in the IRGC navy. This force is backed up by some 350,000 trained reservists. The IRGC-controlled Basij, a paramilitary militia that provides for internal security, provides 100,000 men, with another two million (and possibly six million) upon full mobilization.[cxliii] The army fields over 1,660 tanks (including some 480 modernized T-72s), nearly 8,800 artillery pieces of all types, and over 220 helicopters. The air force has some 240 high-performance combat aircraft in service, including 35 MiG-29s and 44 F-14 Tomcats. The Iranian navy fields 15 submarines, including three Russian-built *Kilo*-class boats, six missile-armed corvettes and 24 missile-armed fast-attack craft. There are also about 50 midget submarines that have mine-laying capability. The IRGC navy has some 40 missile-armed combatants, along with a considerable number of small boats organized in flotillas.[cxliv] Iran also has some 400 anti-ship missiles, including 100 C-801/802s. Some 25-30 vessels carry the C-802, and another 60 are deployed on Qeshm Island, just inside the Strait of Hormuz.[cxlv] Mines number 3,000, including 100 rocket-propelled EM53s.[cxlvi]

Iran also provides support to non-state actors across the globe. Most important is Hezbollah, centered in south Lebanon. With $100 million annually in Iranian aid and an IRGC training mission, Hezbollah now fields tens of thousands of rockets and missiles, as well as UAV's that have entered Israeli airspace. It has also sent guerilllas and terrorists to Venezuela, and has been reported to have a presence in Mexico, with the potential for action in North America and Western Europe. Palestinian groups like Hamas and PIJ have also received Iranian support, as have Shia groups in Iraq and Yemen.[cxlvii]

Most dangerously, Iran possesses a considerable ballistic missile force, under IRGC control, which includes 400 Scud, 90 Shahab-3 and 18 BM-25 surface-to-surface missiles. The Shahab-3 has a range of between 1,300-2,000 km., enough to reach the Mediterranean. The BM-25, developed by North Korea, has a range of 2,500 km., and there are reports that its range is being extended to 3,500 km.[cxlviii] Iran is also believed to be developing the Shahab-5, which has a 6,000 km. range, enabling it to reach targets anywhere in Europe.[cxlix]

Iran's strategic doctrine has been geared toward closing off the Persian Gulf to outside (namely U.S. and Western) forces.[cl] In 2007, Ayatollah Khamenei, who is commander-in-chief of Iran's armed forces, gave Iran's navy responsibility for operations outside the Gulf and the IRGC navy the primary role in it. The IRGC's doctrine is similar to that outlined in 1999 by Rear Admiral Ashkbous Danekar (before the 2007 delineation). This includes: naval and amphibious assaults on enemy bases and installations, utilizing islands in the Gulf; blocking oil-shipping routes; carrying out attacks with commandos on enemy oil facilities; utilizing fast missile boats, anti-ship missiles and mines, as well as offensive electronic warfare; and making the Gulf of Oman the first line of defense.[cli] Iran's navy, according to Khamenei, is to be a "strategic navy." This would mean, according to Iranian naval officials, that Iran's navy would deploy in strength in the Indian Ocean (between the Strait of Hormuz and the Strait of Malacca) and the Red Sea (between the Strait of Bab al-Mandeb and the Suez Canal.)[clii] Iran's air force would also play an important role in this doctrine. In their 2010 study of the Iranian Air Force, Tom Cooper, Babak Taghvaee and Liam F. Devlin note that "The air force is also equipped to exercise effective control over most of the Persian Gulf, the Strait of Hormuz, as well as large parts of the Gulf of Oman. Under the given circumstances, and also in the face of future challenges, the IRIAF [Islamic Republic of Iran Air Force] remains a force to be reckoned with."[cliii]

All of this presents the United States and its allies with a formidable challenge in the event of war. In a recent article, Joseph Miranda noted the dangers facing Western states in a conflict with Iran:

"...a Coalition victory against Iran would necessarily be predicated on the war being kept limited to the Persian Gulf and its environs, as well as its being over relatively quickly, before the inescapable disruption it caused to the oil market drove the global economy into recession. Otherwise, were such a conflict to spread too far or last too long--for example, involving new militant regimes in Islamic states created by further Arab Spring-type uprisings...the...Coalition would find itself with a vastly changed strategic situation. The resultant disruption of the globalized economic and political network might then prove to be a vulnerability that again brought forward an older form of large-scale warfare."[cliv]

North Korea: The North Korean People's Army consists of over a million men on active duty, plus 600,000 reservists. It fields some 3,500 tanks, 21,000 artillery pieces and several hundred surface-to-surface missiles. The air force operates over 600 combat planes, while the navy has nearly 400 surface ships and 72 submarines.[clv]

On the whole, the North Korean forces are equipped with obsolete or ageing weapons, and the country's disastrous economic and demographic situation has had an adverse effect on its military. However, Pyongyang does have an advantage in that it would determine when hostilities would be initiated. Furthermore, much of North Korea's artillery is within range of Seoul, which would cause enormous casualties and damage at the outset of a war. Its special forces, some 180,000 strong, also provide a means of causing disruption ahead of a full-scale invasion, while its submarine force--as shown by the sinking of the *Cheonan* in 2010--could cause serious problems for South Korean and U.S. naval forces.[clvi]

The other key threat from North Korea are its ballistic missiles and WMD. Some 750 ballistic missiles are operational, and some can be counted on to have WMD warheads. These would cause enormous casualties if used against South Korea, and create panic as well.[clvii] North Korea's Taepodong-1 ballistic missiles easily range over Japan, while the Taepodong-2 has a range of 6,000km., enough to reach the continental United States.[clviii] The Musudan road-mobile intermediate-range missile was tested in April 2013. While their actual range is not certain, U.S. official sources indicated that they could have a range of up to 4,000 km., which could reach U.S. bases in Guam.[clix]
A second Korean War, initiated by Pyongyang, would thus cause not just massive destruction and loss of life on the Korean Peninsula, but also have serious consequences, both geopolitical and economic, on a global scale.

Venezuela: Since Hugo Chavez came to power in 1998, the country has become an adversary of the United States. Large-scale arms purchases from Russia have been made for its 115,000-strong armed forces. These include T-72 tanks, SA-15 surface-to-air missiles and 24 fifth-generation Su-30 fighters.[clx] Venezuela has also been building up its forces along its border with pro-American Colombia. This has included a mechanized brigade with Russian armored vehicles just 13km. from the border, while another brigade has received Russian heavy mortars.[clxi] Although small, the navy has three submarines, six missile-armed frigates and three missile-armed patrol craft.[clxii] These could mount hit-and-run attacks on U.S. ships in the Caribbean, while army units, cooperating with FARC, could make incursions into Colombia, drawing U.S. forces away from other areas.

Russia: In recent years Russia has moved to rebuild its decrepit military after the long post-Soviet decline. Russia's defense budget doubled between 2006 and 2009, from $25 billion to $50 billion, while that for 2013 is listed as $90 billion.[clxiii] Its armed forces have some 845,000 personnel on active duty, supported by a reserve of two million more.[clxiv] They field some 2,550 main battle tanks, over 16,000 armored fighting vehicles, and over 5,400 artillery pieces. The air force has nearly 1,250 tactical combat aircraft, 400 transport aircraft and some 1,000 helicopters, while the navy deploys 85 tactical submarines and more than 30 major surface warships, including an aircraft carrier.[clxv] As noted above, Russian strategic forces are being upgraded, and the conventional branches too are being restructured and re-equipped. The army is now being organized into brigades, akin to the U.S. Army, and is receiving new tanks and armored vehicles like the T-90 main battle tank, of which 1,600 are in service. These have both reactive armor and an electromagnetic pulse weapon to immobilize an enemy's electronics.[clxvi] Airborne forces are being increased by three air-assault brigades, improving Russia's ability to rapidly deploy forces to crisis areas, while special task force brigades, along with marine and special operations units, are to be included in Russian rapid deployment forces. Special operations capabilities are to be unified (as they are in the U.S. military) by the creation of a Special Operations Command, which will be part of the reserve directly under President Putin's control, as Supreme Commander-In-Chief.[clxvii]

The navy is slated to receive $160 billion for modernization through 2020. Four French-built *Mistral* amphibious ships are joining the fleet, increasing its power projection capabilities. Plans call for 10 Project 885 *Yasen*-class submarines to be delivered by 2020, and four are under construction. According to the Russian press, they are reputed to be stealthier than even U.S. subs and will carry more firepower, including new Onyx supersonic cruise missiles.[clxviii] The Yakhont supersonic cruise missile (which has been sold to Syria) and Shkival torpedo (sold to Iran) likewise add to the firepower and lethality of the Russian fleet.[clxix] The SS-N-27 anti-ship missile is especially worrisome. Used in sea-, air- and ground-launched variants, this missile has a 300 km. range and reaches speeds of up to 3,000 km. per hour in its last minute of flight (from about 15 km. from the target.), allowing it to cover this distance in less than 20 seconds. Given that it flies at about 100 feet, the SS-N-27 is very difficult to detect.[clxx]

The air force has also been modernized with fifth-generation fighters. As many as 300 Su-34 Fullback strike aircraft are planned to be deployed by 2022, along with another 300 Sukhoi Pak fighters.[clxxi] The KH-102 air-launched cruise missile has a range of 1,800 miles and accuracy to within 50 feet, and has both nuclear and conventional capability.[clxxii]

In the realm of cyber warfare, Russia has also been improving its capabilities. It is believed that Russia's massive cyber warfare program is state-sponsored, and targets military, economic and commercial networks with cyber attacks. It has been used to infiltrate both foreign and domestic networks that are determined to be threats to Russia's interests and security.[clxxiii] Nor are official networks the only ones utilized. According to an article published in the Winter 2014 *inFocus Quarterly* by cyber expert David J. Smith, "Russia--its government and a motley crew of sometimes government-sponsored but always government-connected cyber-criminals and youth group members--has integrated cyber operations into its military doctrine." This relationship between the government and what Smith describes as a "thriving cyber-criminal industry," as well as pro-government youth groups, has led to a situation that "In sum, Russia--in its capabilities and its intent--presents a major cyber challenge to the United States."[clxxiv]

In addition to asserting itself in Ukraine and in the Middle East, Russia has been building up a presence in Latin America. Russia has had a close relationship with Venezuela, conducting port visits and joint naval exercises and deploying two long-range nuclear-capable Tu-160 Blackjack bombers to a Venezuelan airbase in October 2013.[clxxv] Russia is supplying arms to Brazil, including 12 Mi-35 attack helicopters, and will soon deliver Pantsir-S1 and Igla-S surface-to-air missiles.[clxxvi] Russia has established warm relationships with left wing and often anti-American leaders in Ecuador, Argentina and El Salvador, and in October 2013 signed a memorandum of cooperation with Nicaragua's Sandinista government. Russian forces have been given permission to train Nicaraguan forces, and will engage in joint naval patrols with Nicaraguan forces for six months beginning in January 2015.[clxxvii] Moscow has also begun to improve cooperation with its old ally, Cuba. In February 2014, the Russian intelligence ship *Victor Leonov* reportedly made an unscheduled visit to Havana harbor. Its armament included surface-to-air missiles and 30mm guns.[clxxviii] It reportedly carried out surveillance of the U.S. ballistic missile submarine base at Kings Bay, Georgia, as part of a Russian nuclear exercise in April.[clxxix]

Russia has supplied hundreds of modern combat aircraft to such countries as China and Venezuela, along with large quantities of tanks, vehicles, helicopters and missiles to these and other states hostile to the United States.

China: China too is engaged in a major military buildup. China's armed forces, the People's Liberation Army (PLA) number some 2,333,000, equipped with over 6,800 main battle tanks, 7,800 armored fighting vehicles, over 13,000 artillery pieces, nearly 2,100 tactical combat aircraft, more than 700 helicopters, 66 general purpose submarines and 70 major surface warships.[clxxx] The defense budget has increased exponentially. In March 2014, Beijing announced that its defense budget had been increased by 12.2 percent over last year's, which would make the figure $132 billion. Despite the view of numerous experts that this figure is too low (actual expenditures are estimated to be twice that, at $260 billion, with a total of $400 billion if other ministries involved in defense activities and paramilitary forces are included), this represents a public indication of the importance China places on increasing its military capacity.[clxxxi]

The PLA has also been modernizing its training and doctrine. Chinese military planning emphasizes the integration of land, naval, air and missile forces in operations, while the 2013 White Paper emphasizes "warfighting capabilities based on information systems," which in American terms means that C4I2 (Command, Control, Communications, Computers, Intelligence and Information) is now a primary goal for the PLA.[clxxxii] Multi-division exercises by the army and large-scale aerial training involving multiple aircraft types indicate the importance the PLA places on ensuring that its forces are capable of utilizing new equipment effectively.[clxxxiii]

Most striking is its naval modernization. An aircraft carrier, the *Liaoning*, has been procured, which made three deployments in the Yellow Sea in 2011. In April 2013, China formed its first carrier escort group, consisting of two destroyers, two frigates and a supply ship. These ships appear to be similar to U.S. destroyer and replenishment ship designs. The *Liaoning* is expected to operate 24 fighters, most probably Su-30s. The Chinese plan to build at least another four carriers for their navy. Moreover, China has held major fleet exercises, in April 2010 and June 2011. The 2011 exercise saw 11 ships, including three missile destroyers and four frigates, pass within 110 km. of Okinawa. The exercise also included submarines and UAVs.[clxxxiv] In July 2013, Chinese warships moved through the La Perouse Straits, which separate Russian Sakhalin and Japan. Chinese warships--again for the first time--made a complete circuit around the Japanese home islands. Also in 2013, for the first time in history, Chinese warships transited the Strait of Magellan during a visit to Chile and Argentina, while at the same time a Chinese amphibious ship with marines aboard visited Syria, the first time China had sent that type of ship to the Mediterranean. In February 2014, Chinese warships transited the Sunda Strait, between Java and Sumatra, again for the first time.[clxxxv] The Chinese navy has undertaken major exercises that have improved its capabilities, double the number five years ago.[clxxxvi]

Most significant has been the deployment of the DF-21D anti-ship ballistic missile, specifically designed for use against U.S. carriers. Its range is between 1,500-2,000 km., with a speed of 7,680 mph. It is believed to have control system that allows it to be maneuvered in the final stage of flight to its target. Given China's stated interest in expanding its influence in the South China Sea, such a weapon could force the U.S. Navy to keep its carriers back from threatened areas, giving China a decisive sea-denial advantage.[clxxxvii]

Other Chinese missiles have been modernized. The YJ-62 Silkworm anti-ship missile is now being fitted to China's latest destroyers and is being exported (as the C-602) to Pakistan and Burma. The YJ-62's range is 400 km., and it can spot targets at a range of 40 km. and confirm them at 30 km.[clxxxviii]

China is also building up its air force. In 2014, China fielded 148 Su-27/30 fighters, along with 205 J-11's, a Chinese variant of the Su-27.[clxxxix] Its own industries have been building modern aircraft as well. The J-10 (similar to the Israeli Lavi fighter that was cancelled in the 1980s), which entered service in 2004 is equipped with a digital fly-by-wire system and a "look down/shoot down" radar comparable to Western fighters.[cxc] Some 220 are in service.[cxci] Its first stealth fighter aircraft, the J-20, was flown in 2011 with a service date of around 2018.[cxcii] It has enhanced tail and vertical fin features, allowing it's radar signature to be reduced, while its twin engines provide considerable thrust and speed.[cxciii] The J-20 is also reported to have a heavier weapons payload than the F-35 Joint Strike Fighter, allowing it to carry heavy anti-ship missiles. As a report by the on-line security website Lignet notes, "A mass-produced, stealthy fighter-bomber would enable the Chinese air force to evade enemy radar, attack an adversary and eliminate their command and control nodes, anti-aircraft missile sites and radar installations. This would allow China to make a larger follow-on attack from the air that could be devastating."[cxciv]

An even more advanced design is the Wu-14, a hypersonic glide vehicle. First noted as being in testing by U.S. intelligence on January 9, 2014, the Wu-14, described as "a hybrid cruise/ballistic missile carried atop the last stage of a larger ballistic missile," was launched into "near space" and released at 80,000 feet, then flew several thousand miles, toward China, at an estimated speed of Mach 10, or 7,612 mph. The Wu-14 gives China a major advance in hypersonic weapons technology, as well as the ability to carry out air strikes against distant enemies with much greater ease.[cxcv]

These developments show just how far China has come in a short time in developing a modern air force, one which will be of growing importance in the next few years.[cxcvi]

China's longer-range missiles have been improved. Not only is its nuclear arsenal been modernized, but dual-capable missiles are being deployed that could put U.S. bases at risk of Chinese attack. The Dong Feng (DF)-26C intermediate-range ballistic missile (IRBM) has the range to strike Guam, vital to the U.S. military posture in the Western Pacific.[cxcvii] Moreover, China's close ties with Russia have included missile technology. In April 2014, Russia's President Putin signed off on an agreement for the export of S-400 missiles to China. These are a potential game-changer in the military balance in Asia, as the S-400s can intercept both ballistic and cruise missiles and aircraft. They could help establish Chinese air superiority over the Taiwan Strait, and can be deployed near the Senkakus, inhibiting Japan's ability to maintain control of the air space over the contested islands. Moreover, they could nullify India's shorter range nuclear missiles, weakening India's deterrent capability *vis a vis* China, given recent border disputes between the two countries.[cxcviii]

This has gone hand-in-hand with a policy of expanding Chinese influence in areas of importance to the United States. In Latin America, China has been actively promoting the sale of sophisticated weaponry to many nations in the region, including those hostile to Washington. Ecuador, Bolivia and Venezuela have procured Chinese equipment, with its fourth generation J-10 fighter being offered to Venezuela, Peru and Argentina. At a recent exposition in Peru, China included a 22,000-ton amphibious assault ship and its new *Yuan*-class attack submarine.[cxcix] In the Middle East, China has established close relations with Iran. In March 2013, Iranian and Chinese warships carried out joint exercises from the port of Zhangjiagang.[cc] Both countries also have cooperated on the production of anti-ship missiles. In February 2012, Iran began producing the Zafar cruise missile. According to a report for the U.S.-China Economic and Security Review Commission, the Zafar is "a short-range, antiship, radar-guided missile apparently based on [sic] Chinese C-701AR missile."[cci] Iran is believed to be manufacturing other Chinese anti-ship missiles under license, including the C-401, C-802 and C-803.[ccii]

China has also deployed its naval forces in the 200-mile Economic Exclusion Zones (EEZ) of the United States. In May 2013, at a security conference in Singapore, Admiral Samuel Locklear, Commander-in-Chief of the U.S. Pacific Command, confirmed that a Chinese officer had disclosed that these incursions had occurred. While Locklear did not disclose the locations, it is believed that they involved transits by Chinese ships and submarines near Guam.[cciii] According to Larry Wortzel, a retired military intelligence official whose specialty is China, Beijing has also sent intelligence ships into U.S. EEZs off Hawaii, as well as Guam, leading to speculation that China's position on the existing Law of the Sea agreements, in relation to naval deployments, may be changing.[cciv]

There has also been growing confrontation on the high seas between U.S. and Chinese naval forces. In December 2013, a Chinese warship sailed within 100 yards of the U.S. guided-missile cruiser *Cowpens*, which was monitoring the carrier *Liaoning* in the South China Sea. This was reportedly the most serious naval incident between the two fleets in several years.[ccv]

More recently, China's use of its improved cyber warfare capabilities, carried out against both U.S. military and civilian sectors, has become widespread. According to a recent Pentagon report, this effort is aimed at collecting information for improving China's military. However, it also noted that "military cyberspace capabilities...appear designed to enable anti-access/area-denial...missions (what PLA [People's Liberation Army--the Chinese armed forces] strategists refer to as 'counter-intervention operations') and that "Chinese EW [Electronic Warfare] strategy stresses that it is a vital fourth dimension to combat and should be considered equally with traditional ground, sea, and air forces."[ccvi] China is believed by many experts to be the world's foremost practitioner of cyber warfare. Not only has it hacked into U.S. systems, including defense networks, corporations and research facilities, but it has reportedly hacked Indian government networks, Australia's intelligence apparatus and Canadian government departments.[ccvii] Indeed, U.S. Congressional panels have declared that China presents the greatest existing threat to the digital security of the United States.[ccviii] Combined with a growing anti-satellite capability,[ccix] this portends a greater threat in areas that the United States has been secure in since the end of the Cold War.

With China's navy deploying as far afield as the Indian Ocean and Red Sea, its interest in securing access to raw materials,[ccx] and its growing military capabilities, Sino-American rivalry, akin to the U.S.-Soviet rivalry of the Cold War, is a distinct possibility.

Conclusion.

The world is entering an era of growing confrontation, with the possibility of major war increasingly probable. The emergence of rival great powers, even with only regional capabilities, has challenged America's heretofore secure global position, along with that of the existing international order. More dangerously, the expansion of radical Islam over the past few years, with its desire to destroy the West, has increased the possibility of armed conflict exponentially. The diffusion of sophisticated weaponry and WMD to many of these states, and their links to terrorist groups with messianic aspirations, means that even the costly but limited conflicts of the 2000s are unlikely to be repeated. The Red-Green alliance has meant that battlefronts are once again global, and our enemies can project their power into areas of vital interest for us on a worldwide scale.

The rising great powers, Russia and China, which see themselves as adversaries of the United States, have likewise begun to challenge the existing international system. Russia's actions in Georgia in 2008 were an early indicator of this, and its support for the Assad regime in Syria, along with its diplomatic maneuvers on behalf of Syria in 2013 regarding its chemical arsenal and Iran in 2014 in its nuclear negotiations, exemplify Moscow's assertion of itself as a power that is taking a stand against the West. Most recently, its annexation of the Crimea and its intimidation of Ukraine (which includes large-scale military deployment on its borders and unrest in the eastern regions of that country), along with its designs on Moldova and the Baltic States, mark a clear example of a confrontational policy meant to reassert Russian power.[ccxi]

China, for its part, has likewise been behaving in an increasingly bellicose manner toward its neighbors. China has long held what is known as the "nine-dash line claim," which encompasses nearly all of the South China Sea, an area of 1.4 million square miles, almost to the shores of the Philippines and Malaysia.[ccxii] This is part of China's objective of controlling of the Spratly Islands, rich in energy and mineral deposits, which China claims as being part of its territory. In 2012, Chinese forces took control of the Scarborough Shoal, part of the Philippines, and they are currently blocking Philippine access to the Second Thomas Shoal. China has also provoked conflict with Japan over the Senkaku Islands, which have large undersea oil deposits nearby.[ccxiii] In 2013, China established an Air Defense Identification Zone over the seas off its east coast, which included parts of Japan and South Korea[ccxiv] Most recently in May 2014 a fleet of some 80 Chinese ships sailed into an area south of the disputed Paracel Islands, well within Vietnam's 200-mile wide EEZ. They installed an oil rig in the area and then, when confronted by Vietnamese naval vessels demanding that the rig be removed, rammed several of these ships, injuring at least six Vietnamese sailors.[ccxv] Given the long history of conflict between the two countries in this area (as well as their bloody border war in 1979), this could easily become a flashpoint for regional war, given the multiple claims in the South China Sea and the increasing alarm that China's neighbors have over Beijing's actions.[ccxvi]Beijing's confrontations with India over border demarcation are further examples of China's rise as a hostile power in a region of vital importance to global security and prosperity.

The actions taken by Russia and China are even more worrisome given that these two great powers are moving toward ever closer cooperation. Both countries have engaged in joint naval exercises, and Russia's Putin and Chinese President Xi Jinping will hold a summit meeting in May 2014. This is expected to lead to the signing of an agreement for the construction of a gas pipeline from Russia to China and to improve military cooperation, particularly in arms and technology transfers. These agreements come as both countries are engaged in expansion that is at the expense of their neighbors, and the West is divided and increasingly ineffectual in world affairs. As a recent Lignet report notes, "Perceived weakness in both Europe and the United States has created a power vacuum that Moscow and Beijing are willing and eager to fill...If the new relationship evolves into a grand alliance, it would be the most significant geopolitical shift since the breakup of the Soviet Union in 1991."[ccxvii]

The large-scale efforts by both Russia and China to expand their military capabilities give their actions credibility. So too for the states that constitute the core of the Red-Green alliance, Iran, North Korea and Venezuela. While some of these states have the capacity to act effectively in other areas of coercion--namely Iran and Venezuela regarding energy prices--it is their ability to project military power--both directly and through proxies--that constitutes their primary threat to the West.

From the standpoint of defense, the reasonable response to these developments would be to initiate a major modernization of the U.S. armed forces, replacing ageing and obsolescent weapons and equipment and maintaining numerically large and flexible forces to meet these growing threats. However, the opposite is the case. Under Barack Obama, the United States is neglecting its armed forces, dangerously reducing their size and eroding their capabilities at the same time that our enemies and rivals are increasing theirs. The dangerous policies toward the nuclear deterrent endanger not only American global leadership but also our physical security, since many emerging nuclear powers-- namely Iran and North Korea--that have a desire to cause serious harm to the United States, have shown they have no intention of reversing or eliminating their arsenals or efforts to acquire them.

Most seriously, Obama's solicitous approach to America's adversaries, especially in the Islamic world, has led to an official view that the United States no longer faces the possibility of war. Obama's approach to this issue is, like so much else in his presidency, an attempt to consign the recent wars to the past, and his predecessor, conveniently ignoring the fact that conflict is not only continuing, but is likely to escalate, thanks to his policies. Russia's actions in the Ukraine, China's belligerence in the Western Pacific and the continued hostility of states like Iran and Venezuela expose the bitter fruit of Obama's abandonment of traditional American diplomacy, of standing with allies and against foes, and of maintaining a credible military posture for deterrence.

Obama's muddled and self-defeating policies have emboldened our adversaries and aroused contempt. North Korea's belligerence in 2013, together with the embarrassing revelation that the United States lacked the necessary anti-missile interceptors to prevent North Korean missiles from striking the Continental United States, is a case in point. While the administration reversed course and announced additional interceptor deployments, these will not be accomplished for several years. Given the pace of North Korean missile development, this could see a dangerous window of vulnerability opened. So too has Obama's approach to the safety and security of uniformed Americans. The reprehensible response to Fort Hood and Benghazi, along with the various statements about trying U.S. service personnel in foreign courts for alleged war crimes, are only the most egregious examples of this attitude.

The massive cuts in defense spending that have been underway over the past several years have served to undermine even the administration's signature strategic policy: the so-called "pivot" to Asia, which would see U.S. forces in the Pacific increased substantially in order to counter China's growing military capabilities and its bellicose actions. In November 2011, a hitherto secret program, known as the Air Sea Battle Concept, was unveiled by the Pentagon. This would see the Navy, Marine Corps and Air Force combine their forces in order to defeat what were described as "anti-access and area denial weapons," akin to those being deployed by China.[ccxviii] As developed, Air Sea Battle is highly ambitious. It calls for U.S. forces to take any war with Beijing to the Chinese heartland. China's anti-satellite launch sites would be attacked, in order to prevent Chinese forces from disrupting American space-based systems, while submarine bases would also be knocked out. Furthermore, U.S. special forces would conduct raids on Chinese missile bases, and there would even be efforts, thorough covert action, to stir up unrest among minority groups in Xinjiang, Tibet and in Inner Mongolia. All the while, U.S. forces would engage in combat in the Western Pacific meant to defeat Chinese naval, air and missile forces.[ccxix]

By any standard, this is an impressive strategy, and one that calls for large and flexible U.S. forces to carry out.[ccxx] However, the budget cuts that have been in effect since 2010 have made the successful implementation of Air Sea Battle highly problematic. Among the weapon systems necessary for Air Sea Battle would be a new long-range bomber, which has been planned for some time. Given the continued reductions in defense spending, and the long lead time needed to develop and deploy such an aircraft, it will be a long time in coming. The same is true for long-range UAV's.[ccxxi]

Moreover, the effects on existing force levels undermine the efficacy of Air Sea Battle. With the Navy at fewer than 300 ships and with its carrier and cruiser forces likely to fall as a result of the FY 2015 budget, the sea power that is central to the success of this strategy will likely not be available. Indeed, the news that the U.S. Navy will not have a deployed carrier in the region for up to four months in 2015 renders this strategy impotent for that time.[ccxxii] The rundown of procurement of the Tomahawk cruise missile will mean that the ability to strike at targets deep within China will be questionable, while the fall in Air Force strength, particularly tactical combat aircraft, further erodes confidence in the ability to carry out these plans.

All these factors led to an important slip by the Obama Administration regarding the overall "pivot" strategy. In early March 2014, Assistant Secretary of Defense Katrina McFarland said in a speech that "Right now, the pivot is being looked at again because, candidly, it can't happen," due to the lack of funds for it to be carried out. Although the Obama Administration and the Pentagon quickly "clarified" her statement, McFarland reiterated what she had said, and insisted that she was simply stating what Secretary Hagel had said about having to make due with fewer assets.[ccxxiii]

This has led to a questioning of the commitment by the United States to support its allies in the face of Chinese aggression. The April 2014 treaty with the Philippines is a case in point. At a press conference in Manila, Obama praised the treaty, but then indicated that the United States was not committed to militarily defend the Philippines. Given the lack of a strong response to China's earlier actions[ccxxiv] (with the exception of sending single bomber flights through China's air defense zone), together with the reductions in U.S. military capabilities, this hardly makes the American commitment seem credible to allies or adversaries.[ccxxv]

The situation in Asia is simply one example of the adverse effects that American military retrenchment has had for the international system. The possibility that Saudi Arabia might arm its ballistic missiles with nuclear warheads is an example of the growing loss of confidence in Washington's ability to provide a credible military deterrent for its allies.

In Europe, the emergence of Russia's growing assertiveness, backed up by military power, has led NATO to look to its defenses after nearly a quarter century of post-Cold War neglect. With the danger of Russian interference in or intimidation of such NATO allies like the Baltic States and Poland, there has been a growing realization that the Alliance simply does not have the means to defend itself without American help, given the lack of training and planning for combined operations among European NATO states.[ccxxvi] In a May 2, 2014 speech, Secretary Hagel called for NATO members to spend at least two percent of GDP on defense, while at the same time singling out Russia as the most serious challenge to the Alliance due to its actions in Ukraine.[ccxxvii] However, given the downward trend in defense spending and forward deployment by the United States, as well as continued reductions and reluctance by the European members to take up the slack, a robust military posture by the Alliance seems increasingly unlikely.[ccxxviii]

Even some within the Obama Administration have realized the dangers of the present approach, despite their implementation of the policies that have caused these dangers. At a press conference announcing the cuts for FY 2015, Secretary Hagel stated that, given both the concurrent reductions in U.S. force posture and the growing capabilities of our adversaries, "we are entering an era where American dominance on the seas, in the skies, and in space can no longer be taken for granted." While he followed up with a standard statement on doing more with less, Hagel was forced to admit that "However, as a consequence of large budget cuts, our future force will assume additional risk in certain areas."[ccxxix] Hagel's predecessor, Leon Panetta, has also warned of these dangers. Writing in the *Wall Street Journal* on April 30, 2014, Panetta noted the multiple dangers to American security from such states as Russia, Iran, China and North Korea, and while praising the Obama Administration for such actions as killing Osama Bin Laden, warned that "While a mood of withdrawal and restraint is spreading in both political parties, recent events suggest that the U.S. may need to address crises around the world that threaten our national security. Our military must be prepared to respond if necessary."[ccxxx] He further noted that

"For diplomacy to succeed, it must be supported by a strong and credible defense. Now is not the time to weaken our military, but that is exactly what is happening...After every major conflict in recent history, deep defense cuts, 'hollowed out' the military. Troops were not adequately trained or equipped, maintenance was delayed, and key investments were postponed. A U.S. at peace has meant a U.S. without a military that can respond effectively to crisis."[ccxxxi]

Increasingly, the situation we are facing is similar to that of 1979. Major reductions in spending over several years had significantly eroded the capabilities of the U.S. armed forces. The Soviet Union had been increasing the size and effectiveness of its military, thanks to nearly 15 years of steady investment. The world had become a much more dangerous place, and would become even more so as a result of anti-American revolutions in Iran and Nicaragua and the Soviet invasion of Afghanistan. A vacillating and indecisive president, who had championed a new era of peaceful cooperation with our adversaries was now forced to reverse this policy and to take a firm stand as a result of these events. The American people, weary of war and international responsibility, now realized they faced a myriad of increasing dangers to their security from sworn enemies abroad. Indeed, the threat of superpower confrontation was very real by 1980, given the growing instability in the international system and the growing imbalance of power. Thanks to decisive American leadership and a major investment in U.S. military strength in the early-1980s, the United States was able to restore a favorable balance, and also helped bring about the eventual collapse of Soviet Communism within a decade.

Indeed, one of the similarities between today's situation and that of 35 years ago is the nature of our adversaries' strength. As mentioned above, it is through the projection, both directly and indirectly, of military power. The disastrous economic situation in the states constituting the Red-Green Axis--Iran, North Korea and Venezuela--has led to increasing instability within and to a realization among neighboring states (Saudi Arabia and the Gulf states regarding Iran, for example) that these nations pose a danger to their security, which has led to major efforts to improve military capacity. Even the great power rivals, Russia and China, face economic uncertainty, due to sanctions (Russia) and an overheating economy in an unstable international economic environment (China), meaning that the projection of military power has become more important for the assertion of national influence. China's bellicose actions in the South China Sea, with its deposits of petroleum and other natural resources, is an example of this. Likewise, the Soviet Union, in 1979-80, was faced with a similar situation. As Edward Luttwak wrote at the time,

"Once these factors [economic and ideological decline] are admitted into the overall picture, the danger of conflict is greatly heightened. If military advantage prompts activism, in the search for ways of exploiting power otherwise perishable, and if a transitory advantage adds the urgency of a time limit to that intent, the combination of a short-lived military optimism with a long-term regime pessimism is a most powerful impulse to war--in the attempt to change an unfavorable future by forceful action."[ccxxxii]

Such a danger is magnified by the enormous reductions in investment and force structure by the United States, particularly when combined with the lack of concurrent investment by other Western states in their defenses. Given that U.S. defense spending is projected to increase again in the early 2020s, when many of the delayed weapon systems will start to come on line, this too gives our adversaries a limited time in which to use their military might to gain a geopolitical advantage. This also combines with the uncertainty regarding American leadership after 2016. Given the track record of Obama's foreign policy, this means that somewhat less than three years remain in which our adversaries will be able to move with certainty of a weak American response and a diminishing capacity on the part of the West--especially the United States--to counter their objectives.

To quote Luttwak (who cited Austria-Hungary in 1914 and Japan in 1941 as examples), "[T]here is no more certain driving force to deliberate war than the conjunction of short-term military optimism and long-term national (or regime) pessimism."[ccxxxiii] This summarizes very succinctly the situation that our adversaries face today.

The obvious question that arises from this is: What is to be done?

Given that we are in the middle of a second Obama term, it is difficult to imagine that, short of a scenario like the one described at the start of this report, that much can be done. However, there are correctives that can be taken.

First, Congress must act to prevent additional defense cuts and reverse those that have been made. This is particularly true of the FY 2015 budget, which goes into effect in the fall. The Republican majority in the House must make a firm stand against the elimination of such vital weapons as the A-10 and the Tomahawk, as well as the reductions in naval strength. While a minority in the Senate, Republicans there too must join in the fight. Given that many Democrats are now uneasy about the direction our military readiness is taking, some level of bipartisanship on this issue (which existed in 1979-80 regarding the Soviet threat) is possible. The increasing bellicosity of our adversaries in Ukraine and the South China Sea, together with Iran's and North Korea's continued development and deployment of nuclear weapons, should give Congress the necessary incentive to press forward. A good starting point for Republicans on this issue would be the preamble to the Constitution, which charges government to "Provide for the Common Defense." Moreover, it also directs government to "Promote the General Welfare," not to *provide* for it, which is what Obama appears to believe and has provided enormous sums of money to do.[ccxxxiv] Such a message, well thought out and delivered, will shape public perception on this issue.

A second area where change can be affected is in educating the public on the dangers that the United States faces, and the consequences of the decline in military capability that is underway. Congressional Republicans must of course make this an issue, and so must all who care about America and the preservation of freedom in the world. A sound alternative to the Obama Administration's policies would be a rebuilding of American military strength that would allow for the deployment of U.S. forces in strength against any of our adversaries in any part of the globe. A return to the two-war strategy, centered on simultaneous conflicts in the Middle East and Asia (either another Korean war or Chinese action in the Western Pacific), with a reserve of forces for other contingencies (Venezuela in the Caribbean, for example), in conjunction with our allies in NATO as well as in the Middle East (i.e. Israel) and Asia-Pacific (Japan, South Korea, Australia, New Zealand and ASEAN), is needed to counter the dangers we and our allies face today.

Above all, we must remember that history provides clear lessons of the dangers of our present course. The disastrous defeat of the Allies in 1940 nearly led to Nazi domination of Europe and a springboard for world power. So too did the defeats suffered in 1941-42 by America and her allies in the Pacific and Asia at the hands of the Japanese. The beginning of the Korean War in 1950 saw unprepared U.S. forces humiliatingly routed. In all these cases, the lack of preparedness elicited a heavy cost, and the free world only prevailed by a hair's breadth. Given the global reach of our enemies, the nature of military technology (long lead times for development and deployment of weapons) and for proper investment, we cannot again afford to take the chance of defeat, especially since the consequences would be far more terrible than even these past catastrophes.

Let these lessons be remembered.

---

[i] Hanson, Victor Davis. How the Obama Administration Threatens Our National Security, Encounter Broadside, No 5 (Encounter Books, New York, NY., 2009), p. 1.

[ii] Geller, Pamela and Robert Spencer. The Post-American Presidency: The Obama Administration's War on America (Threshold Editions, New York, N.Y., 2010), pp. 109-110.

[iii] Geller and Spencer, pp. 114-115.

[iv] Hanson, pp. 29-30.

[v] D'Souza, Dinesh. The Roots of Obama's Rage (Regenery Publishing, Inc., Washington, D.C., 2010), p. 178.

[vi] International Institute for Strategic Studies (IISS) The Military Balance 2012 (International Institute for Strategic Studies, London, 2012), pp. 44-45; IISS The Military Balance 2013 (International Institute for Strategic Studies, London, 2013). p. 65; IISS The Military Balance 2014 (International Institute for Strategic Studies, London, 2014), p. 35. The request for FY 2013 had initially been $620.2 billion (Military Balance 2013, p. 65.)

[vii] Office of the Under-Secretary of Defense (Comptroller)/Chief Financial Officer, United States Department of Defense, Fiscal Year 2015 Budget Request Overview, March 2014, p. 1-1. This is the "enacted" budget for the current fiscal year.

[viii] Kagan, Frederick W. "The Peril of Sequestration," *National Review*, May 6, 2013, p. 46.

[ix] "US Hollows Out Defense Budget, Asks NATO to Pick Up Slack," http://www.lignet.com/Special Pages/, February 28, 2014; "NATO's Military Decline," *The Wall Street Journal*, March 25, 2014, p. A14. According to the *Journal* article's accompanying statistics, the average for 10 NATO members (Britain, Denmark, Estonia, France, Germany, Greece, Italy, Lithuania, Poland and Spain), came to 1.6 percent of GDP in 2013. While NATO guidelines call for member states to spend 2 percent of GDP on defense, only Estonia, Great Britain and Greece spent more than this level. Overall, the United States contributes 70 percent of NATO spending ("Suddenly, NATO Needs to Spend, But Cash Is Hard to Come By," http://www.lignet.com/SpecialPages/, May 2, 2014.)

[x] McGarry, Brendan. "Defense Budget Would Cut Troop Pay and Benefits," Military. com, February 24, 2014, http//www.military.com/daily-news/2014/02/24/; Sisk, Richard. "Proposed Budget Cuts Benefits, End Strength, Ships," Military.com, February 24, 2014, http://www.miltary.com/daily-news/2014/02/24/

[xi] Geller and Spencer, pp. 215-217.

[xii] Geller and Spencer, p. 226. The extent of Abed's injuries was a "bloody lip."

[xiii] Nor has this been limited to legal matters. As a result of defense cuts, U.S. military personnel and their families in Japan faced cuts in electrical power, which included a shutoff in heating for three weeks at Yokota Air Base in March 2013. "Pentagon Cuts Feared Tripping Up Pivot to Asia," *The Wall Street Journal*, May 4-5, 2013, p. A10.

[xiv] IISS Military Balance 2014, p. 298.

[xv] Spring, Baker. "Obama's Budget Makes Protecting America Its Lowest Priority," Heritage Foundation *Backgrounder*, March 1, 2012, p. 2.

[xvi] Gertz, Bill. "End of American Military Dominance," *The Washington Free Beacon*, February 25, 2014, http://freebeacon.com/endofamerican-military-dominance/

[xvii] Spring, pp. 3-4.

[xviii] "US Hollows Out Defense Budget, Asks NATO to Pick Up Slack."

[xix] Herman, Arthur. "We Few, We Very Few," *National Review*, March 24, 2014, p. 22.

[xx] Spring, p. 5.

[xxi] Gertz, "End of American Military Dominance."

[xxii] IISS Military Balance 2012, p. 47.

[xxiii] Barnes, Julian E. "Pentagon Lays Out Ways to Slash Spending," *The Wall Street Journal*, August 1, 2013, p. A10.

[xxiv] Cox, Matthew. "Army Must Shed 6 BCTs to Meet Proposed Budget Cuts," Military.com, February 28, 2014, http://www.military.com/daily-news/2014/02/28. In 2016, there will be 32 BCT's, a dozen fewer than now. While most divisions will have three BCT's (and the Hawaii-based 25th Infantry Division four), the 1st Infantry Division, assigned to the U.S. Africa Command, will have two (IISS Military Balance 2014, p.32.)

[xxv] "The End Of The American Tank Battalion," StrategyPage.com, April 1, 2014, http://www.strategypage.com/. The Army National Guard retains seven armored brigades, with 28 companies, with 392 M-1s. This, together with active Army companies, will see 952 M-1s in service, down from the present 1,288.

[xxvi] Gertz, "End of American Military Dominance."

[xxvii] Gertz, "End of American Military Dominance"; Spring, p. 4; IISS Military Balance 2012, p. 47.

[xxviii] Spring, p. 4; IISS Military Balance 2012, p. 47.

[xxix] "Tank Transports Dying of Old Age," StrategyPage.com, April 28, 2013. http://www.strategypage.com/

[xxx] "Pentagon Budget Cuts Benefits, End Strength, Ships."

[xxxi] Herman, p. 22.

[xxxii] "Pentagon Budget Cuts Benefits, End Strength, Ships."

[xxxiii] Ibid. Hagel declared that "The Active Army will transfer Blackhawk helicopters to the National Guard, where they will bolster the Guard's needed capabilities in areas like disaster relief and emergency response."

[xxxiv] Barnes, p. A12.

[xxxv] Kagan, p. 43.

[xxxvi] Cohen, Steve. "America's Incredible Shrinking Navy," *The Wall Street Journal*, March 21, 2014, p. A13.

[xxxvii] Polmar, Norman. "Counting Warships," *Proceedings*, May 2014, p. 158. These come under the heading of "battle force ships," which consist of aircraft carriers, surface warships (cruisers, destroyers and frigates), small patrol vessels (littoral combat ships and combat craft), submarines (attack, guided and ballistic missile), amphibious ships, mine warfare ships, logistics vessels and auxiliaries. The total number of vessels comes to 289, when five frigates of the Naval Reserve are included.

[xxxviii] Truver, Scott C. and Holzer, Robert. "U.S. Navy in Review," *Proceedings*, May 2013, p. 60.

[xxxix] USNI News Editor. "Navy: Lincoln Refueling Delayed, Will Hurt Carrier Readiness," February 8, 2013. http://news.usni.org

[xl] USNI news Editor. "Down to One Middle East Carrier," February 6, 2013. http://news.usni.org; Kagan, p. 42.

[xli] Kagan, p. 43.

[xlii] Osborn, Kris. "Carrier Refueling Yanked From Unfunded Priorities," Military.com, April 4, 2014, http://www.military.com/daily-news/2014/04/04. The overhaul would take five years and cost $7 billion.

[xliii] Slattery, Brian. "Navy Acknowledges Growing Readiness Concerns," The Foundry: Conservative Policy News Blog from the Heritage Foundation, January 15, 2013. http://blog.heritage.org

[xliv] Polmar, Norman. The Ships and Aircraft of the U.S. Fleet, 19th Edition (Naval Institute Press, Annapolis, MD., 2013), p. 3.

[xlv] Spring, p. 5.

[xlvi] Report to Congress: Navy Combatant Vessel Force Structure Requirement, January 2013, Prepared by OPNAV N8 2000 Navy Pentagon, Washington, DC 20350-2000.

[xlvii] Osborn, Kris. "Navy Unlikely to Reach 300-Ship Fleet by 2020," Military.com, April 4, 2014, http://www.military.com/daily-news/2014/04/04.

[xlviii] Ibid.

[xlix] Lehman, John. "The Seas Are Great but the Navy Is Small," *The Wall Street Journal*, April 26, 2012. http://online.wsj.com/article/

[l] Lehman, April, 26, 2012.

[li] Osborn, Kris. "CNO Tells Congress the US Needs 450-Ship Navy," Military.com, March 12, 2014, http://www.military.com/daily-news/2014/03/12.

[lii] Polmar, 19th Edition, p. 3.

[liii] Military Balance 2014, pp. 45-46; The Ships and Aircraft of the U.S. Fleet, 18th Edition (Naval Institute Press, Annapolis, MD., 2005), p. 2. This number was at 28 in 2013, but increased with the addition of two additional ships by the following year (Polmar, 19th Edition, p. 2.)

[liv] Gertz, "End of American Military Dominance."

[lv] Polmar, 19th Edition, pp. 108, 110.

[lvi] Barnes, August 1, 2013.

[lvii] Sisk.

[lviii] IISS Military Balance 2012, p. 48.

[lix] Lehman. April 26, 2012.

[lx] Gertz, "End of American Military Dominance."

[lxi] Ibid.

[lxii] Cavas, Christopher P. "US Navy Budget Takes Bite Out of Aircraft, Weapons," *Defense News*, March 4, 2014, http://www.defensenews.com/article/20140304.

[lxiii] Ibid.

[lxiv] Ibid. JSOW-C procurement was to be 1,799; it now stands, under the proposed FY 2015 budget, at 400. Procurement of AMRAAM medium-range air-to-air missiles will be suspended in 2015, while the numbers of Standard SM-6, Rolling Airframe and Evolved Sea Sparrow Missiles, along with Mk 48 heavyweight and MK 54 lightweight torpedoes to be added will also be reduced.

[lxv] Ibid. The Navy is planning to establish a "recertification line" in order for the effectiveness of current Tomahawk missiles to be maintained.

[lxvi] Bender, Jeremy. "Raytheon Calls Its Tomahawk Cruise Missile The 'Transformer Of Modern Weapons,'" *Business Insider*, March 5, 2014, http://www.businessinsider.com.

[lxvii] Larter, David. "CNO: Cutbacks reducing Navy's surge readiness," *Navy Times*, April 7, 2014, http://www.navytimes.com/article/20140407/.

[lxviii] Sisk, Richard. "Struggle Ahead to Reach 8-Month Sea Deployments," Military.com, April 8, 2014, http://www.military.com/daily-news/2014/04/08.

[lxix] Axe, David. "Budget Squeeze Forces Carriers Rethink," *Warships International Fleet Review*, March 2014, p. 3.

[lxx] Slattery, January 17, 2013.

[lxxi] Cropsey, Seth. Mayday: The Decline of American Naval Supremacy (Overlook Duckworth, New York, NY, 2013), p. 126.

[lxxii] Herman, p. 22.

[lxxiii] Bendikova, Michaela. "Will the Air Force of the Future Be Capable of Flying?" The Foundry: Conservative Policy New Blog from The Heritage Foundation, January 11, 2013. http://blog.heritage.org

[lxxiv] Spring, p. 5.

[lxxv] Kagan, p. 42.

[lxxvi] Kagan, p. 43.

[lxxvii] Deptula, David A. "America's No-Fly Zones Are Already in Place," *The Wall Street Journal*, June 24, 2013, p. A9.

[lxxviii] Spring, p. 5.

[lxxix] IISS Military Balance 2012, p. 48.

[lxxx] Bendikova, January 11, 2013.

[lxxxi] Eaglen, Mackenzie and Eric Sayers. "U.S. Air Force Fifth-Generation Fighter: The F-22A Raptor Requirements Retreat," Webmemo #2539, The Heritage Foundation, July 13, 2009. http://www.heritage.org/research/reports/2009/07/u.s.-air-force-fifth-generation-fighter-the-f-22a-raptor-requirements-retreat

[lxxxii] Bendikova, January 11, 2013.

[lxxxiii] Babbin, Jed. How Obama is Transforming America's Military from Superpower to Paper Tiger Encounter Broadside No. 14 (Encounter Books, New York, NY. 2010), p. 22. The Navy and Marine Corps estimated a shortfall of 240 fighter aircraft over the same period.

[lxxxiv] IISS Military Balance 2013, p. 50. The Navy will procure 41 F-35B and 37 F-35C aircraft over the period FY 2013-2017, 69 fewer than previously planned.

[lxxxv] Spring, p. 5.

[lxxxvi] Harper, Jon. "Air Force to Eliminate Nearly 500 Aircraft," *Stars and Stripes*, March 12, 2014, http://www.military.com/daily-news/2014/03/12.

[lxxxvii] Harper, Jon. "Air Force Leaders Detail Force Cuts," *Stars and Stripes*, March 15, 2014, http://www.military.com/daily-news/2014/03/15.

[lxxxviii] Harper, "Air Force Leaders Detail Force Cuts"; Boot, Max. "Defense Budget Incoherence," *Commentary*, February 24, 2014, http://www.commentarymagazinecom/2014/02/24. Sequestration would also mean a delay in the Navy's procurement of the F-35's carrier-based variant for two years" (Boot.)

[lxxxix] Boot.

[xc] Thompson, Loren. "Some Disturbing Facts About America's Dwindling Bomber Force," *Forbes*, August 16, 2013, http://www.forbes.com/siges/lorenthompson/2013/08/16/. This is the IOC, or Initial Operating Capability," which as Thompson points out, does not mean full deployment, estimated to be, according to Air Force requirements, some 80-100 aircraft.

[xci] Ibid. In July 2013, Defense Secretary Hagel, as a result of the Sequester, announced that this number could fall to 150,000. The Marines have announced a willingness to reduce their force level to 175,000 if necessary. (Barnes, Julian E. "Branches of Military Battle Over Shrinking U.S. War Chest, *The Wall Street Journal*, August 1, 2013, p. A10.)

[xcii] Boot.

[xciii] Dunnigan, James. "Too Few Good Men," Dirty Little Secrets, December 26, 2012. http://www.strategypage.com/dls/articles/Too-Few-Good-Men-12-26-2012.asp

[xciv] Ibid.

[xcv] Ibid.

[xcvi] Ibid.

[xcvii] Polmar, 19th Edition, p. 205.

[xcviii] Polmar, 19th Edition, p. 207.

[xcix] "US Hollows Out Defense Budget, Asks NATO to Pick Up Slack."

[c] "Harrier Rescues the F-35B," StrategyPage.com, June 4, 2013, http://www.strategypage.com.

[ci] Polmar, 19th Edition, p. 275; Morrison, Samuel Loring. 'U.S. Naval Battle Force Changes 1 January 2012-31 December 2012," U.S. Naval Institute *Proceedings*, May 2013, p. 110. The other Maritime Prepositioning Squadrons (MPS) are MPSRON-2 at Diego Garcia, in the Indian Ocean, and MPSRON-3, at Guam and Saipan in the Western Pacific. The five ships of MPSRON-1 are now berthed at Blount Island and at Newport News, VA, and are classified as having Reduced Operating Status (ROS).

[cii] USNI News Editor. "Twenty Former Marine Generals Want More Money for Amphibs," March 27, 2014, http://www.news.usni.org/2014/03/27. For some top commanders, these levels remain well below what is thought to be needed. Admiral Greenert, speaking to the Navy League in April 2014, stated that "Frankly, we need about 50 amphibious gray hulls to get done what we need to around the world today." Cox, Matthew. "Navy Wants More Ships to Expand Mobile Sea Basing," Military.com, April 7, 2014, http://www.military.com/daily-news/2014/04/07.

[ciii] Kagan, p. 43.

[civ] Spring, p. 6.

[cv] Gertz, Bill. "Obama to Announce Major US Nuclear Force Cuts Soon," *Newsmax*, May 15, 2013, http://www.newsmax.com.

[cvi] Ibid.

[cvii] Polmar, 19th Edition, pp. 59, 61.

[cviii] Polmar, 19th Edition, p. 61.

[cix] Gertz, "Obama to Announce...," Polmar, 19th Edition, p. 59.

[cx] "US Strategic Nuclear Forces Under Financial Attack," Lignet, January 13, 2014, http://www.lignet.com/SpecialPages.

[cxi] Ibid.

[cxii] Gertz, "Obama to Announce..."

[cxiii] Ibid.

[cxiv] Spring, p. 6.

[cxv] Polmar, 19th Edition, pp. 59-60. As Rear Admiral Joseph Tofalo, the Navy's director of undersea warfare, noted in April 2014, "At present, SSBN's operated by the United States Navy submarine force have over half of our nation's deployed nuclear warheads on them. We have a lot at stake here and have to get this right." Osborn, Kris. "Admiral: Crimea Proves Nuclear Subs Still Needed," Military.com, April 7, 2014, http://www.military.com/daily-news/2014/04/07.

[cxvi] Under New START, the U.S. Navy's SSBN force will be equipped with 70 percent of the United States' deployed nuclear warheads. (Osborn, "Admiral: Crimea Proves Nuclear Subs Still Needed.")

[cxvii] Payne, Keith B. "Minimum Deterrence, More Danger," *National Review*, May 6, 2013, p.49.

[cxviii] Gertz, "Obama to Announce..."

[cxix] Military Balance 2014, p. 33. Under New START, the 1,550 level is to be reached by 2018,

[cxx] Spring, p. 7.

[cxxi] "Say Goodbye To More Nukes," StrategyPage.com, April 15, 2014, http://www.strategypage.com.

[cxxii] Gertz, "Obama to Announce..."

[cxxiii] Klein, Joseph. "Russia's Threat in the Americas," FrontPage Magazine, March 28, 2014, http://www.ffrontpagemag.com/2014/. Russia's total inventory was estimated to be 4,500 warheads.

[cxxiv] Ibid.

[cxxv] "Russia Bulks Up Nuclear Arsenal as if Cold War Never Ended," Lignet, October 21, 2013, http://www.lignet.com/SpecialPages/. Since the second Strategic Arms Limitation Treaty (SALT II) of 1979, Russia (both as the Soviet Union and the Russian Federation) has been allowed to maintain heavy ICBMs. Currently, Russia deploys 54 10-warhead SS-18s, though this number may fluctuate depending on future developments regarding Russian defense planning. Military Balance 2014, p. 180.

[cxxvi] Gertz, "Obama to Announce...

[cxxvii] Slattery, Brian. "Russia Sails New Nuclear Submarine While U.S. Continues Fleet Delays," The Foundry: Conservative Policy News Blog from the Heritage Foundation, January 9, 2013. http://blog.heritage.org

cxxviii Lignet, October 21, 2013; "Where Russia Gets It Right," StrategyPage.com, April 22, 2014, http://www.strategypage.com/

cxxix Gertz. Most American tactical nuclear weapons are B-61 bombs carried by F-15Es and F-16C/Ds (Polmar, 19th Edition, p. 59.) Russia, by contrast, is developing new missile systems that have tactical capability. The new RS-26 Rubezh "Frontier" ICBM, has been flight-tested at both intercontinental and shorter ranges, which allows the RS-26 to attack targets in NATO Europe as well as the United States, thus circumventing the 1987 Intermediate Nuclear Forces (INF) Treaty, banning the deployment of intermediate-range nuclear missiles in Europe. Lignet, October 21, 2013.

cxxx Military Balance 2014, p. 33. U.S. tactical nuclear weapons stationed in Europe comprise some 180 B-61 free-fall bombs.

cxxxi "Chinese SSBNs 'Home In' On USA," Warships International Fleet Review, April 2014, p. 9.

cxxxii Gertz; IISS Military Balance 2012, pp. 233-234, 294. The JL-2 has a range of 14,000 km. and is reported to carry either a single warhead or one with 10 multiple warheads ("Chinese SSBNs 'Home In' On USA," Warships International Fleet Review, April 2014, p. 9.)

cxxxiii Ibid.

cxxxiv Ibid.

cxxxv In both Russia and China, the media h lso become more hectoring in its discussions of possible nuclear war with the United States. Stories from Russian television--which often serves as a propaganda arms of the government--include "Topol-M: The Most Powerful Nuclear Weapons in the World," and a TV documentary, "U.S. Nuclear War with Russia," in which U.S. nuclear forces launch a first strike against Russia using SSBNs and bombers, inflicting some 8-12 million casualties ("Russia Bulks Up Nuclear Arsenal as if Cold War Never Ended.") In 2013, China's Communist Party newspaper, Global Times, published maps showing the effects of JL-2 SLBM attacks on the U.S. West Coast, specifically naming Los Angeles and Seattle as targets. The accompanying article noted that such attacks could kill as many as 12 million Americans through blast and fallout (Gertz, Bill. "China Rises as America Weakens," Commentary, May 1, 2014, http://www.commentarymagazine.com/article/china-rises-as-america-weakens/

cxxxvi As Admiral Tofalo noted, "Would Ukraine have resisted the Russian incursion into Crimea if Russia did not have nuclear weapons? It certainly did impact their thinking." Osborn, "Admiral: Crimea Proves Nuclear Subs Still Needed."

cxxxvii "The Mideast Missile Race," The Wall Street Journal, May 2, 2014, p. A12. The DF-3 has a payload of 4,400 pounds and a 1,500-mile range, putting Teheran, which is 800 miles from Riyadh, in easy range. Between 30 and 120 are believed to be deployed. (the IISS Military Balance 2014 (p. 342) estimates 40 missiles on 10 launchers.)

cxxxviii Gertz, Bill. "Saudi Arabia Shows Off Chinese Missiles," The Washington Free Beacon, May 2, 2014, http://freebeacon.com. Henderson also reported that the March 2014 summit between President Obama and King Abdullah was "difficult." The Saudis had in the past assured the United States that the DF-3s, delivered in 1987, would not be armed with nuclear warheads.

cxxxix "The Mideast Missile Race."

cxl As Michael Ledeen has written, "Caracas launders money, transships weapons (as between Russia, Syria and Iran, for example) and drugs, and provides safe havens and training facilities for jihadis, from which they can move toward our poorly defended southern border." "The Big Story--the Global War--Goes Mostly Unreported," PJ Media, March 18, 2014, http://pjmedia.com/michaelledeen/2014/03/18

cxli See my article, "The Unraveling Middle East, Part 2," Frontpage Magazine, March 21, 2011. http://www.frontpagemag.com

cxlii "Crimea May Be Crucial Link in Iranian Chain Reaction," Lignet, March 24, 2014, http://www.lignet.com/SpecialPages/. Russia has also been supporting Iran's nuclear program. In March 2014, Russia agreed to build two additional nuclear power plants and construct new facilities near Iran's nuclear power plant in Bushehr. Russia (along with China) has taken a position contrary to the West's on negotiations, which would allow Iran to maintain most of its 20,000 centrifuges. Rafizadeh, Majid. "Ukraine Crisis Strengthens the China-Iran-Russia Axis," Frontpage Magazine, March 20, 2014, http://www.frontpagemag.com.

cxliii Liebl, Vern. "Oil War: Iran & the Military Balance in the Persian Gulf," Modern War #2, November-December 2012, pp. 15-16.

cxliv Liebl, pp. 16-17; IISS Military Balance 2012, pp. 324-35-25.

cxlv Liebl, p. 17: Dunnigan, James. "Iran Has Two Navies," Dirty Little Secrets, April 24, 2013 http://www.strategypage.com: My article, "Showdown in the Strait of Hormuz," *Frontpage Magazine*, March 7, 2012. http://www.frontpagemag.com

[cxlvi] "Showdown in the Strait of Hormuz."

[cxlvii] Liebl, pp. 17-18.

[cxlviii] Liebl, p. 17: Gold, Dore. The Rise of Nuclear Iran: How Teheran Defies the West (Regenery Publishing, Inc., Washington, D.C., 2009), p. 202.

[cxlix] "The Unraveling Middle East--Part 2." It has not been confirmed if this missile, developed from North Korea's Taepodong 2, has yet been deployed. However, in May 2013, Iran's defense minister, Brigadier General Ahmad Vahidi, displayed 30 transporter-erector-launch vehicles for the country's medium-range missile force (they were displayed at a military parade in September.) This could indicate a strategy--already well-practiced with short-range missiles in exercises--to launch longer-range missiles to overwhelm an enemy's defenses (IISS Military Balance 2014, p. 301.)

[cl] Iran's force of midget submarines is a major part of this. The IS-120 *Ghadir* is equipped with a retractable outboard electric motor which provides added maneuverability, and carries two Shkival torpedoes, which have a high speed and are very capable. A prototype of a 1,200-ton sub, named the *Besat* (or *Qaaem*) has also been built, while the *Fateh*, lead ship of a 600-ton class, is reported to have a new propulsion system, four 533mm torpedo tubes (which can hold Shkivals), and mines. The *Sabehat*-15 Swimmer Delivery Vehicle (SDV) is capable of reconnaissance, mine and special operations missions in coastal waters. (Ansari, Usman. "Rise of the Iranian Midgets Poses a Big Threat to Meet," *Warships International Fleet Review*, April 2014, p. 10.)

[cli] IISS Military Balance 2013, p. 361.

[clii] ISS Military Balance 2013, p. 362. Iran's navy has also been venturing further afield. Early in 2014, an Iranian destroyer and supply ship deployed in the Mediterranean as the first leg of a deployment in the Atlantic. While officially a goodwill mission, the fact that Iran sees the Atlantic as an area for deployment could indicate that Iranian surface warships and submarines, equipped with anti-ship and even cruise missiles could deploy off the U.S. East Coast, threatening U.S. military and civilian targets and shipping lanes, which could also be jeopardized by mines. "Iranian Warships Deploy to Atlantic," *Warships International Fleet Review*, March 2014, p. 2.

[cliii] Cooper, Tom, Babak Taghvaee and Liam F. Devlin. IRIAF 2010: The Modern Iranian Air Force (Harpia Publishing, Houston, TX., 2010), p. 15. Tim Ripley, in his Middle East Air Power in the 21st Century (Pen & Sword Aviation, Pen & Sword Books, Ltd., Barnsley, South Yorkshire, 2010), p. 91, assessing Iran's air power capabilities, notes two major advantages: "Mass (the sheer size of the Iranian air force and its airbase infrastructure means it would take a significant campaign to neutralise it); The size of the country, which would present even the USA with a major challenge for any air space dominance effort." Given the reductions in U.S. air capabilities since 2010, and possible future reductions, these factors remain important in considering the role that Iranian air power would play in a potential Middle East war.

[cliv] Miranda, Joseph. "Target Iran, Part I: US Intervention Doctrine & Strategy," *Modern War*, #10 (March-April 2014), p. 15.

[clv] IISS Military Balance 2012, pp. 257-258.

[clvi] Jonasz, Maciej. "Drive on Pyongyang: Battlefield Korea," *Modern War*, #5, May-June 2013, pp. 8-9, 12-14. The sub that sank the *Cheonan* was an MS-29 *Yono*, which is similar to Iran's IS-120 *Ghadir* (Ansari.)

[clvii] Jonasz, p. 14.

[clviii] Jonasz, p. 14: Minnich, James M. The North Korean People's Army: Origins and Current Tactics (Naval Institute Press, Annapolis, MD., 2005), p. 71: "The Unraveling Middle East--Part 2."

[clix] IISS Military Balance 2014, pp. 215-216.

[clx] IISS Military Balance 2012, pp. 405-406. Russia has also supplied 51 helicopters (40 Mi-17 gunship/transport, three Mi-26 heavy transports, and eight Mi-35 gunships. It is also believed that hundreds of air-to-air, anti-ship and cruise missiles have been purchased by the air force, while the army has received 100,000 AK-103 assault rifles, the latest version of the Kalashnikov (March, David. "Focus on the Venezuelan Army Today," *Modern War* #7, September-October 2013, p. 74.

[clxi] IISS Military Balance 2012, p. 362. A helicopter battalion has also been created near the border.

[clxii] IISS Military Balance 2012, p. 405.

clxiii Osborn, Kris. "Russia Offers Different Threat than Cold War Era," Military.com, March 20, 2014, http://www.military.com/daily-news/2014/03/20.

clxiv IISS Military Balance 2014, p. 180. The active totals are divided among the services as follows. Army, 250,000; Navy, 130,000; Air Force, 150,000; Strategic Deterrent Forces, 80,000; Command and Support, 200,000. There are a further 519,000 paramilitary troops, mainly for internal security, border guard and communications security (pp. 190-191.)

clxv IISS Military Balance 2014, pp. 181-186.

clxvi "Russia Bulks Up Nuclear Arsenal as if Cold War Never Ended." Some 2,300 examples of the T-99, a more advanced tank, will be delivered from 2020.

clxvii IISS Military Balance 2014, pp. 161-163.

clxviii "Russia Bulks Up Nuclear Arsenal as if Cold War Never Ended." Given that these are Russian press reports, the actual capabilities of this class is not yet known. However, it is believed that the Yasen-class boats are comparable to the U.S. Seawolf class, which entered service in the late-1990s. Two Seawolf boats are in service (the Seawolf and Connecticut), along with an improved sub, the Jimmy Carter (See Polmar, 19th Edition, pp. 77-81 for a full description of the Seawolf class.)

clxix IISS Military Balance 2012, p. 187: My "Sea Change for American Power," Frontpage Magazine, June 29, 2012. http://www.frontpagemag.com. The Yakhont can be fired from land, air and sea platforms. "Russia Bulks Up Nuclear Arsenal as if Cold War Never Ended."

clxx "U.S. Navy Hurries Preparations For War With China," StrategyPage.com, July 12, 2013. http://www.strategypage.com The SS-N-27 is deployed aboard Kilo-class attack submarines, including those of China and India. Given Iran's close relations with both Moscow and Beijing, and its own fleet of three Kilo boats, it is not inconceivable that these missiles could at some point be deployed by Iran as well.

clxxi IISS Military Balance 2012, p. 197: Carroll, Conn. "Morning Bell: Obama Just Made Us More Vulnerable...Again," The Foundry: Conservative Policy News Blog from the Heritage Foundation, July 22, 2009. http://blog.heritage.org. The Su-34 has a range of 2,500 miles and can carry eight tons of precision-guided weapons. "Russia Bulks Up Nuclear Arsenal as if Cold War Never Ended."

clxxii "Russia Bulks Up Nuclear Arsenal as if Cold War Never Ended."

clxxiii "Major Cyber War Powers," StrategyPage.com, March 13, 2014, http://www.strategypage.com.

clxxiv Klein.

clxxv Ibid. Four Russian warships visited Venezuela in August 2013, according to the Venezuelan press.

clxxvi Ibid. The Igla-S is a shoulder-fired missile.

clxxvii Ibid.

clxxviii Ibid.

clxxix Gertz, Bill. "Pentagon: Russian Spy Ship, Tug Operating Near U.S." The Washington Free Beacon, April 25, 2014, http://freebeacon.com/

clxxx IISS Military Balance 2014, pp.231-236. The Army has 1,600,000 personnel, the Navy 235,000, the Air Force 398,000 and the Strategic Missile Forces 100,000. There are also 660,000 paramilitary troops and an estimated reserve of 510,000

clxxxi Gertz, Bill. "China Rises as America Weakens."

clxxxii IISS Military Balance 2014, p. 208.

clxxxiii Ibid. As the authors note, "Complex, multi-service exercises such as the Jinan Military Region's 'Joint' exercises between 2006 and 2010 have improved area air-defence and anti-submarine capabilities, as have new ships and aircraft." (Ibid.)

clxxxiv "China Forms Its First Carrier Escort Group," StrategyPage.com, April 23, 2013. http://www.strategypage.com/: "Sea Change for American Power."

clxxxv "The Chinese Navy Goes Global," StrategyPage.com, April 22, 2014. In March and April 2013, a four-ship flotilla consisting of the destroyer Lanzhou, the frigates Hengshui and Yulin and the landing ship Jinggangshan, carried out a deployment in the South China Sea. This included a well-publicized amphibious assault exercise aimed at seizing a small island--indicating that the Chinese navy has the ability to engage in such actions in the region--and a ceremony at James Shoal, which marks the southernmost limit of the area claimed by China in that body of water. Rielage, Dale C., Captain, USN. "Fit to Fight," Naval Institute Proceedings, April 2014, p. 55.

clxxxvi IISS Military Balance 2014, p. 208. The authors point out that "coastal-defence operations by land-based anti-ship cruise missile, aviation, surface and sub-surface forces are practiced routinely." (Ibid.)

clxxxvii Cropsey, p. 169: "Sea Change for American Power."

clxxxviii "Silkworm Goes Long," StrategyPage.com, April 23, 2014. The C-602's range is 280 rather than 400 km. and has some differences in electronics, mainly countermeasures. Both versions have a 300 kg. (660 pound) warhead.

clxxxix IISS Military Balance 2014, p. 236; Rupprecht, Andreas and Tom Cooper. Modern Chinese Warplanes: Combat Aircraft and Units of the Chinese Air Force and Naval Aviation (Harpia Publishing, Houston, TX., 2012), pp. 71-76. Another 24 Su-30s and 48 J-11s serve with naval aviation (IISS Military Balance 2014, p.235.)

cxc Rupprecht and Cooper, pp. 66-70.

cxci IISS Military Balance 2014, pp. 235-236. Another 24 serve with naval aviation.

cxcii IISS Military Balance 2012, p. 212.

cxciii "China Finds Fastest Way to Develop a Stealth Fighter: Steal It," Lignet, March 26, 2014, http://www.lignet.com/SpecialPages/

cxciv Ibid. The report notes that "Parity in the skies between an American stealth jet and a similar Chinese airplane can be overcome by superior pilots using better tactics and maneuvers. But if the J-20 is as good as intelligence analysts think it is, then China enjoys a strategic air advantage over its neighbors--a worrisome security development in the Far East."

cxcv Gertz, "China Rises as America Weakens." Gertz notes that U.S. investment in hypersonic technology was just $36 million in 2013, with this figure reduced in the current budget, although Congress will probably increase funding.

cxcvi IISS Military Balance 2012, pp. 238, 212.

cxcvii Gertz, "China Rises as America Weakens."

cxcviii "Putin OKs Advanced Antimissile Sale to China: Report," Global Security Newsline, April 11, 2014, http://www.nti.org/

cxcix Gertz, Bill. "Rising Red tide: China encircles U.S. by sailing warships in American waters, arming neighbors," The Washington Free Beacon, June 7, 2013. http://www.washingtontimes.com/

cc Klein, Joseph. "Mideast Red Star Rising," Frontpage Magazine, June 12, 2013. http://frongpagemag.com

cci Ibid.

ccii IISS Military Balance 2013, p.360.

cciii Gertz, June 7, 2013.

cciv Ibid.

ccv Gertz, "China Rises as America Weakens."

ccvi "New Pentagon Report Shows China Preparing for War," Lignet, June 4, 2013. http://www.lignet.com/

ccvii "Major Cyber War Powers."

ccviii Ibid. A case in point is China's J-20 stealth fighter. In 2007, Chinese cyber warfare experts assigned to the Technical Reconnaissance Bureau (believed to be part of the PLA's Integrated Network Electronic Warfare), were able to steal classified design data--through the use of a computer virus or worm that enabled them to take control of computer operating systems--on the F-35 Joint Strike Fighter, which were used in the development of the J-20. According to a March 26, 2014 report by Lignet, an on-line security website, "The J-20's capabilities caught up to the F-35 with astonishing speed. The J-20 now mounts the latest electro-optical targeting system under its nose, similar to the F-35's configuration, which gives Chinese pilots a better field of view." Lignet notes that, whereas the F-35 "has been delayed for years and is now 70 percent over budget, " the J-20 went from "a demo version in 2011 to a flying prototype in several phases over the past two years." "China Finds Fastest Way to Develop a Stealth Fighter: Steal It."

ccix See Dunnigan, James. "The Chinese Conspiracy in Orbital Space," StrategyPage.com, June 21, 2013. http://www.strategypage.com

ccx Miranda, Joseph. "Red Dragon Green Crescent: Naval Warfare in the 21st Century," Modern War #1, p. 15.

ccxi In addition to its regular armed forces, Russia also has a major asset in the form of its Main Intelligence Directorate, known by its Russian acronym GRU. Established during the Soviet era, it maintains most of the mandates it had during that time, including intelligence gathering and its own special forces units, known as Spetsnaz. There is credible information that points to the use of Spetsnaz units in the recent takeover of the Crimea and in fomenting unrest in eastern Ukraine. According to a recent Lignet report, the

GRU's 45th Spetsnaz Regiment have been active in both areas, whose objectives are to "start brawls, recruit pro-Russian militants, persuade Ukrainian soldiers to change sides, supply arms to separatists and otherwise fan the flames of unrest." "Russia's GRU: Sleeper Agents Behind the Masks in Ukraine," Lignet, May 7, 2014, http://www.lignet.com/

[ccxii] Osborn, Kris. "Carlisle: China's Aggressive Stance on Islands Causes 'Concern,'" DoDBuzz, May 5, 2014, http://www.dodbuzz.com/2014/05/05; "China Clashes With Two Neighbors at Sea," *The Wall Street Journal*, May 8, 2014, p.A1.

[ccxiii] China has also made claims on Okinawa, with the above mentioned naval deployments and earlier, in 2004, the deployment of a submerged Chinese submarine, tracked by U.S. and Japanese naval forces. In addition to oil, the Senkakus have large deposits of fish, with Chinese fishing boats taking 150,000 tons annually. "Island War In The Pacific," StrategyPage.com, May 2, 2014, http://www.strategypage.com/

[ccxiv] Gertz, "China Rises as America Weakens"; Glick, Caroline B. "Column One: Life under the Obama Doctrine," *The Jerusalem Post*, May 1, 2014, http://www.jpost.com/

[ccxv] Spegele, Brian, Vu Trong Khanh and Josephine Cuneta. "Ships Clash Over China's Sea Push," *The Wall Street Journal*, May 8, 2014, p. A8; "China Answers Obama," *The Wall Street Journal*, May 9, 2014, p. A14. According to Rear Admiral Ngo Ngoc Thu, commander of Vietnam's coast guard, at least seven Chinese warships were present, along with aircraft.

[ccxvi] According to James Hardy, Asia-Pacific editor at IHS Jane's Defence Weekly, "Vietnam has a record of not pulling back from military confrontations" (Spegele, et. al.)

[ccxvii] "Russia-China Ties Could Lead to Seismic Geopolitical Shift," Lignet, May 14, 2014, http://www.lignet.com/SpecialPages/

[ccxviii] Gertz, Bill. "China's High-Tech Military Threat," *Commentary*, April 1, 2012, http://www.commentarymagazine.com/ This coincided with Secretary of State Hillary Clinton's article in that month's issue of *Foreign Policy*, meant also to deter North Korea. It also involved the adoption of a Bush Administration plan to station 60 percent of U.S. naval forces in Asia (Gertz, "China Rises as America Weakens."). This will see the number of ships deployed in the Pacific rise from the current (2014) total of 52 to 65 by 2020 (Holzer, Robert D. and Scott C. Truver. "U.S. Navy in Review," *Proceedings*, May 2014, p. 66.)

[ccxix] Ibid. U.S. aircraft carriers would be defended from Chinese ballistic missiles (like the DF-21D) some 1,000 miles from Chinese territory. According to Seth Cropsey (p. 280), Air Sea Battle "knits together air force and navy aircraft, allied bases, a hardening of support functions throughout the western Pacific, and increased attention to defending against ballistic missiles in the service of blunting China's ability to deny U.S. seapower access to the region in the event of hostilities."

[ccxx] For additional reading on Air Sea Battle, the author recommends in addition to the sources cited: Greenert, Admiral Jonathan W., USN and General Norton A. Schwartz, USAF. "Air-Sea Battle," *The American Interest*, February 20, 2012, http//www.the-american-interest.com/articles/2012/air-sea-battle/; Kline, Jeffrey E. and Wayne P. Hughes, Jr. "Between Peace and the Air-Sea Battle: A War at Sea Strategy," *Naval War College Review*, Autumn 2012, Vol. 65 No. 4; Tol, Jan van. "AirSea Battle: A Point-of-Departure Operational Concept," Center for Strategic and Budgetary Assessments, May 18, 2010, http://www.csbaonline.org/publications/2010/05/airsea-battle-concept/4/

[ccxxi] Ibid.

[ccxxii] Glick.

[ccxxiii] Gertz, "China Rises as America Weakens."

[ccxxiv] Glick.

[ccxxv] When Air Sea Battle was announced in 2011 (and in a May 2013 report), the authors of the strategy went to considerable lengths to not mention China as the adversary that the strategy was directed against. A variety of foreign military capabilities were included in the concept, including small boat "swarm" attacks, a specialty for Iran's naval forces (Forman, David, Commander, USN. "The First Rule of Air-Sea Battle," Naval Institute *Proceedings*, April 2014, p. 27.)

[ccxxvi] "A European Tragedy," StrategyPage.com, May 6, 2014, http://www.strategypage.com/

[ccxxvii] Sisk, Richard. "Hagel Wants More NATO Spending to Counter Russia," Military.com, May 2, 2014, http://www.military.com/. According to Hagel, "Over the long term, we should expect Russia to test our alliance's purpose, stamina and commitment." NATO Deputy Secretary General Alexander Vershibow noted that "Clearly, the Russians have declared NATO an adversary, so we have to begin to view Russia no longer as a partner but as more of an adversary than a partner."

[ccxxviii] Under current plans, just 30,000 U.S. military personnel will remain in NATO Europe, compared to 10 times that number at the end of the Cold War. Moreover, most will be support troops, as nearly all U.S. combat formations have been withdrawn. In March 2013, for example, the last 22 M-1 Abrams tanks were shipped back to the United States, ending 69 years of U.S. armor deployment in Europe. "The Americans Are Gone," StrategyPage.com, April 10, 2013, www.strategypage.com/

[ccxxix] Gertz, "End of American Military Dominance."

[ccxxx] Panetta, Leon E. "Playing Politics With Military Readiness in a Dangerous World," *The Wall Street Journal*, April 30, 2014, http://online.wsj.com.

[ccxxxi] Ibid.

[ccxxxii] Luttwak, Edward N. On the Meaning of Victory: Essays on Strategy (Simon and Schuster, New York, 1986), p. 267. Luttwak further noted that "Thus if, by war, the Soviet Union could achieve a permanent enhancement of its position in some decisive map-changing way, all would become easier in the future...Alternatively, successful warfare might seize valuable resources for the Soviet state, and then the advantage of such resources might serve to modify the future that now looms so unfavorable" (ibid.)

[ccxxxiii] Ibid.

[ccxxxiv] As Bruce Thornton has pointed out, "The claim that we cannot 'afford' a larger military is preposterous. The same week Hagel announced the cuts, Obama proposed spending $302 billion on roads. In 2013 defense spending was 4% of GDP, while mandated entitlement spending and interest payments on the debt were 14.5%...half the amount of the $1 trillion in the 2011 budget sequester cuts are coming from defense, while the real engines of our debt and deficits, Social Security, Medicare, and Medicaid, were left untouched. We have the money, but we just choose to spend it on ourselves rather than on ensuring that we have the military power to defend our security and interests." "Sacrificing the Military to Entitlements," FrontPage Magazine, March 3, 2014, http://www.frontpagemag.com/2014/bruce-thornton/sacrificing-the-mil...